"*Tender Warrior* is a very meaningful and enlighte.... .... any man to read who is interested in seeking to become a man in the full sense of the word. Stu Weber certainly has captured the dilemma that many men find themselves in in today's society, and outlines strategies for becoming more fully human and also more fully Christ-centered in their lives."

TOM OSBORNE, HEAD FOOTBALL COACH-UNIVERSITY OF NEBRASKA
(NATIONAL CHAMPIONS 1994)

"*Tender Warrior* is a must read for every man seeking true masculinity, written in a style that is easy to understand and apply. From the viewpoint of a member of the profession of arms, Stu Weber is credible. He has been there and paid his dues. I recommend the book as a manual for a men's accountability group."

ROBERT L. VERNON, ASSISTANT CHIEF OF POLICE
LOS ANGELES, (RET.)

"These are the two most helpful books written for men in the last five years."
(*Tender Warrior* and *Real Men Have Feelings Too* by Gary Oliver)

H. NORMAN WRIGHT, BEST SELLING AUTHOR AND NATIONAL SPEAKER

"When Stu Weber wrote *Tender Warrior,* he unintentionally wrote an auto-biography. Never have I read a book which has more credibility in terms of the author's own life. In a day when our culture is at once confused and concerned over gender identity, men everywhere would do well to recalibrate their personal compasses by the Biblical benchmarks found in *Tender Warrior.* I highly recommend this book!"

DR. BRUCE H. WILKINSON, PRESIDENT AND FOUNDER
WALK THRU THE BIBLE MINISTRIES

"This is a book of encouragement. In a day where the meaning of the word loyalty has been lost, Stu Weber reminds us as men, especially in chapter four, to exercise staying power."

COACH BOBBY BOWDEN, FLORIDA STATE FOOTBALL
(NATIONAL CHAMPIONS 1993)

"Weber is particularly good at showing how times of tension are potential learning experiences that can either be grasped or unwittingly passed by. Weber demonstrates a keen ability to weave a tale and turn a phrase."

BOOKSTORE JOURNAL

TENDER WARRIOR

GOD'S INTENTION FOR A MAN

STU WEBER

TENDER WARRIOR
© 1993 by Stu Weber

Published by Multnomah Books
a part of the Questar Publishing Family

Edited by Larry R. Libby
Cover Design by David Uttley

Printed in the United States of America

International Standard Book Number: 0-88070-579-5 (hardback)
International Standard Book Number: 1-57673-335-1 (paperback)

97 98 99 00 01 02 03 — 10 9 8 7 6 5 4 3 2 1

To
BYRON C. WEBER
my father, my hero…Dad.

And to my three Tender Warriors:

KENT BYRON WEBER
my first-born son
and night owl buddy
who bears his grandfather's name.

BLAKE NATHAN WEBER
my "middle arrow"
and ministry partner
who bears, like the prophet of old,
his own strong name.

RYAN STUART WEBER
my perspective-yielding friend
whose "bear hugs are the best"
and who bears his father's name.

No man could ask for a finer quiver full.
May you impact on target.

AND TO LINDA
my wife, their mother, and the lady
who made us all more tender.
You are the most determined human
being I've ever met.
Thanks, dear! You're an incredible woman.

CONTENTS

Let me shoot straight with you. You are holding in your hands a great book. *Tender Warrior* is a great book because it is written by a great leader. Wherever Stu Weber has gone over the last twenty five years, he has been a superb leader of men. He has led on the football field, behind enemy lines in Vietnam as a member of the Special Forces, in a growing and dynamic church in the Pacific Northwest, and most importantly, he has led his family. It doesn't take much time watching his three sons to realize that these young men were raised by a unique leader.

Tender Warrior is a title that describes the author. You could drop Stu in the middle of a jungle without any tools, weapons, or provisions and he would be just fine. That's toughness. But you can also put Stu into a group of people and it won't take him long to identify the one with a broken heart or a broken dream. That's tenderness. The bottom line is this: Stu is a great leader of men because he is a superb follower of Christ. That's why I like to hang around Stu. I always come away with a little more balance.

In a day like ours when books written to men roll off the presses like cheeseburgers coming through a drive-through window, *Tender Warrior* is a piece of aged and tender New York steak, seared to perfection and sizzling with juices that confirm just the right splash of seasoning.

Many men will read this book. Even more will study this book. But most men will devour this book.

Believe me. It's that good.

STEVE FARRAR
Dallas, Texas

A C K N O W L E D G M E N T S

DON JACOBSON—publisher and friend, who *insisted* this book happen. Thanks, Don, for your belief in me over the years. May your tribe, "partners," and impact increase!

LARRY LIBBY—editor and artist, who *made* this book happen. Thanks, Larry, for your humble spirit and incredible giftedness. They only told me half the story. You are one of a kind...and a friend!

JOAN PETERSEN—my secretary, who keeps me "on the right page" in this crazy, soul-growing calendar called "life in the ministry."

THE MINISTRY MANAGEMENT TEAM AT GOOD SHEPHERD CHURCH (truly "a few good men"):

ALAN HLAVKA—pastor of "see-that-it-gets-done." (Who needs a Franklin planner when you have a Hlavka?)

STEVE KEELS—ministry developer, best student ministry pastor in the Northwest, and "staff entertainer" par excellence.

BOB MADDOX—team trainer and faithful servant, master of the transferable, and the only water polo player I've ever known.

STEVE TUCKER—administrator of integrity and heart, life-saver and friend, whose eye for detail makes us all look good. To put it in your own words, "Thank you."

The encouraging people of Good Shepherd Community Church and my fellow elders—who lead such a "happening" in Oregon's countryside:

ARDEN MEYER	BYRON WEBER
TOM POOLE	NORM NORQUIST
JIM SPINKS	MEL ERICKSON
DENNY DEVENEY	ALAN HLAVKA

You lead the flock so well. We all love you for it.

Wake-Up Call:

A Man Faces Himself

The present time is of the highest importance—
it is time to wake up to reality...
The night is nearly over; the day has almost dawned...
Let us arm ourselves for the fight of the day!
(ROMANS 13:11-12, PHILLIPS).

HOW MANY TIMES can a man hear a wake-up call without waking up? Some men, I suppose, never do. This man almost didn't.

I've had two major wake-up calls at two crossroads in my life. Neither was much like the gentle ring of an alarm clock. Both were more akin to the crack of a two-by-four across the back of my skull. But I guess you could say I hit the "snooze" button twice before coming fully awake.

The first call came in the heat and terror of Vietnam. I was serving in the Fifth Special Forces Group. The last guy who had held my job had just been court-martialed along with five other Green Beret officers who had allegedly crossed a few lines of their own—such as murdering a triple agent. I was the Group Intelligence Operations Officer. In many ways it was a great job. The Berets' AO (Area of Operation) was essentially the entire country. I was responsible for briefing "the old man," Colonel "Iron Mike" Healy, on the enemy situation around our A Team camps from the Delta in the south to the DMZ in the north. Very few young captains had access to the entire country as I did. Very few could grab aircraft when needed. It was heady stuff for a twenty-five-year-old from Yakima, Washington.

One of our functions was associated with flying the SLAR ships—Huey helicopters equipped with Side Looking Airborne Radar. Used to locate enemy troop movement, they flew almost daily. Several of us officers took turns flying with them. On one of the days I was not flying, the ship went down. One of my fellow officers was killed. When the news was confirmed at headquarters, a thick silence descended.

We were all angry. Sick. Frustrated. Sorry it was him. Glad it wasn't us.

Somehow it fell to me to collect his personal effects and prepare them for shipping home to his wife. Such a task makes a guy reflect a bit. As I was cleaning out his locker, it dawned on me that he would never see his wife again. He would never be able to tell her "I'm sorry." For a moment, an uncomfortable thought pricked me…like the tip of a knife blade, just breaking the skin. I knew that I had been living by a "second chance philosophy of life." I had always figured— Hey, if I hurt Linda today, there's always tomorrow. Tomorrow I'll do better.

Now, for my friend, there was no tomorrow.

One little message came scrolling across the screen of my mind. *Okay, Stu. It could have been you. What if it had been you?*

I shook it off. That kind of stuff happened to other people. Other people's choppers went down. Other people died. Not me. What I was actually doing was postponing my wake-up call, pushing it away. The alarm was ringing, but I didn't want to hear it. I punched the "snooze" button and blocked it from my mind.

Some time later, however, the alarm rang again. Louder. Much louder.

It started when I was in midair.

I had just jumped out of an airplane with an officer from II Corps. Ranking soldiers often jump as "wind dummies" so the pilot can observe where they land and adjust to the winds and the DZ (drop zone). That way, the rest of the "stick" (other jumpers) can land where they are supposed to.

As I left the right side of the plane, my partner went out the left. In a freak turn of events we came together under the plane—chest to chest. Instinctively reacting to our training, we pushed away from one another, like marionettes dancing at the end of strings. We cleared, but his chute dropped below me, and I ended up on top of his canopy. Now fully-deployed, his canopy was creating a vacuum that was not allowing my chute to open. As trained, I ran across his canopy and jumped, trying to clear it.

It didn't work.

I tried it again. Still it didn't work.

He landed with me on top of his canopy. It folded around me rendering my landing blind. I "crashed" hard, but the flowing adrenaline covered the pain and we managed to remove the chutes, hide them in the bushes, and wait for the rest of the guys. I was "fine," but something felt peculiar. Something inside my chest wasn't right.

For the next several weeks I was moved from the field, to the dispensary, to the next dispensary, and finally to the hospital facilities at Cam Ranh Bay. The doctors searched for an explanation to the damage. There had to be some kind of weakness to allow the sternum to separate as it did. The most likely reason for that weakness? A malignancy.

What? Saved from a botched parachute jump to die of cancer? How could that be? How could that happen?

Sitting there in the hospital at Cam Ranh, lonely, scared, and homesick, I was forced once again to think about death. My death. In my mind's eye, it was closer than ever before.

As it turned out, there was no malignancy. Only one slightly damaged and very shaken trooper. I healed up, and as before, pushed away any thoughts of my own mortality, and went back to duty.

One more punch on the "snooze" button.

I'd had two chances to respond to the wake-up call. Two chances more than I deserved. Two chances more than a lot of my friends had been given. But God, in His grace, gave me yet one more.

It was in the spring. On a hillside. We were at Dak Pek, at the northern end of the Dak Poko Valley in the central highlands. My face was pushed into the muddy banks of a small trench at the perimeter of a Special Forces A-Camp.

Something was out there. Something big. And we knew it. All the indicators were there. We'd been picking them up for days—more frequent "hostile" contact with our patrols, increased radio traffic (only "big boys" had such radios in the North Vietnamese Army), and a real upsurge in other tactical intelligence in the area. Even the informant "agent nets" began to pick up abnormal numbers of clues.

They were out there all right. And we were their target. Overrunning a Special Forces A-Camp was a prime trophy for any NVA big shot.

It was not pleasant. In some ways, it was almost as bad as being under attack. Just knowing that there were several companies of crack North Vietnamese regulars out there on the perimeter—waiting for the right moment to come screaming out of the forest—turned life into a waking nightmare. There in that muddy ditch—reeling from the fears and threats of imminent combat—I finally heard the wake-up call. I finally faced the real possibility that I would never go home. I finally faced up to the fact that I might not "beat the odds." My life might indeed end in that faraway place. It might not be "someone else" leaving that valley in a body bag. It might not be "someone else" flying home in a silver, flag-draped coffin.

I could actually die. Within hours. Minutes. Seconds. As I grappled with those thoughts, a question burned its way to the surface of my mind. After smoldering in my soul for months, the question now burst into hot flame. What matters? What really matters?

If a young captain by the name of Stuart K. Weber died in the Dak Poko Valley, what would he have accomplished during his quarter century on earth? What was life all about, anyway?

Called back to Nha Trang, I caught a helicopter out of Dak Pek, missing the worst of the battle. Our little camp was virtually blasted from the face of the planet. Eventually, the siege lifted and the NVA crawled away to lick their wounds. Our guys loaded up the wounded, collected the dead, and began to build the camp all over again. Somehow, for some reason, I'd been handed yet one more chance to wake up and open my eyes.

And this time, I did. I began rethinking my life.

Again, I went back to duty. But I was never the same. The spiritual roots of my childhood, long abandoned during the social and intellectual turmoil of the sixties, began to take hold in my heart. The faith of my father and grandfather sent pilings deep into my soul. I realized that Jesus Christ was exactly who He said He was. He became very real to me. Life changed from that day.

Another Kind of Wake-Up Call

Some fifteen years into my marriage with Linda, I experienced my second life-changing wake-up call. It wasn't much less shocking than the first. Another two-by-four. This one didn't come out of the sky like a mortar shell, but it did come "out of the blue." Actually, it flashed out of Linda's eyes. For the first time in all our years together, I saw anger there. Deep anger. Hot anger. It was not like Linda. That made it unmistakable.

It was absolutely clear—there would be some changes in our relationship, or our relationship would change. Things were never going to be the same.

Linda and I had met as kids. She was playing third base on an eighth grade girls' softball team. My sophomore cronies and I were watching the proceedings intently, and not solely out of a burning interest in baseball. During the course of the contest, a hot grounder went to third. Linda scooped it up and in one fluid motion pegged it to first. I was stunned. She didn't "throw like a girl." There was no arch in that peg. It carried all across the infield in one flat trajectory. Whoa! I was impressed. I wanted to know a girl who could compete like that.

A couple of days later I saw her in a print skirt, femininity personified. Now I really wanted to get to know her.

Three years of high school, four years of college, three sons, and twenty-five years of marriage later, we are still together. And in a fun kind of way, I suppose we are still competing.

Linda and I believe that if we can have a meaningful marriage, anyone can. We are both first-borns. We are both aggressive in personality and competitive in nature. She grew up in an abusive home and subconsciously determined never to be dominated by another male. In my early years I was unsettled in my relationship with my mother and subconsciously decided I would never be manipulated by another female. Today we are growing beyond these things. But in the early days of our marriage we were unwittingly speeding toward a washed-out bridge.

At the fifteen-year mark, when I looked into my wife's angry, flashing eyes, I began to realize some things. Seems I had been taking our relationship for granted. Looking back, I realized I had been treating her more like a trophy (conquered and on the shelf) than a companion. More like a contractual partner than a friend with whom to share my insides. The signals had been there, but I hadn't seen them. Typical guy. But this time that "second chance" philosophy was finished. Linda and I began to rediscover one another. We still are.

But how did we come to that morass? Why did marriage shape up in those early years more like combat than companionship? It had a lot to do with my manliness—or the lack of it. Understanding how the living God put me together as a man has helped us grow as a couple.

And manliness is what this book is about. Manliness—real, God-made, down-in-the-bedrock masculinity—is something men in our culture are scrambling to understand. Tough? Tender? Strong? Sensitive? Fierce? Friendly? Which is it? We're frustrated. Often confused. Sometimes irritable. But determined. Determined to discover our manhood and live it to the hilt.

To do that, we first need to look our culture's confusion straight in the eye. We need to look at ourselves and face up to a few things. We need to sort through what really matters in life and go fifteen rounds with some tough issues.

Maybe you've already experienced a couple of wake-up calls in the course of your life.

Lying in a hospital bed with a searing pain in your chest, getting tangled in your buddy's parachute, listening to the whistle of incoming mortar shells, or looking into the furious eyes of the only woman you've ever loved can certainly open a fellow's eyes.

Chances are, you won't need the kind of alarm bells it took to pry me out of slumber. As a matter of fact, our gracious God might even choose to use a book like this to accomplish the same thing in your life, without all that trauma and shock and sheer terror. So…let's consider this your first wake-up call. We have a great day ahead of us, lots of ground to cover, and a mother lode of encouragement just waiting to be mined.

Up and at 'em, Tender Warrior.

A Man Faces Himself

1. Take about thirty minutes to sit down with paper and pen. Divide your life into your major areas of responsibility (husband, father, church, job, friends, etc.). As honestly as you can, ask yourself if you need a wake-up call in any of these areas. Jot down any "problem areas" and note one or two things you could do about them next week.

2. (For the stouthearted): Ask your wife to read chapter 1 of *Tender Warrior* and then ask her, "Hon, if you could name just one area where you think I could use a wake-up call, what would it be?"

A Man Meets with His Friends

1. Just what is a "wake-up call"? Are the wake-up calls described in this chapter common problems with many men? Why, or why not?

2. Have you ever received similar wake-up calls? How did you react? What did you do?

3. At the heart of a major wake-up call is the question, "What really matters?" What really matters to *you*? In what ways do you demonstrate how critical it is to you?

4. What do *you* want to accomplish with your life? When your tombstone is carved, what words do you hope appear on it? What are you doing *now* to ensure that those words might, in fact, appear there?

5. Do you think you need a wake-up call? If so, in what area(s)? If your answer is no, would your wife agree?

6. How would your closest friends describe "manliness"? How would your co-workers? Your boss? Your pastor?

7. Agree or disagree: "It's harder today for a man to be a real man than it is for a woman to be a real woman." Why?

8. Before you read the rest of *Tender Warrior*, describe what you believe it means to be "a man's man."

The Return of Flint McCullugh:

A Man and His Pro-vision

Is there anything worse than blindness?
Oh, Yes! A person with sight and no vision.
HELEN KELLER

I
F YOU WERE GLUED to the tube as I was in the early sixties,
you may remember a western called *Wagon Train*. It always opened
with stocky, fatherly Ward Bond astride his mustang, squinting
wind-chiseled features into the horizon. With a quick look back over
his shoulder, he would raise a rawhide-gloved right hand in a beckon-
ing gesture and call out, "Wagons, *ho-oh!*"

Then the great caravan of canvas-topped prairie schooners bearing
clear-eyed pioneers would begin rolling inexorably behind while the
theme music filled our living room and stirred my young heart with a
thirst for adventure. Ward Bond was perfect as Seth Adams, the gruff,
bluff, but kindhearted wagon master. I loved the way he commanded
that great prairie train snaking its way across the wide plains.

But the guy *I* really wanted to see came galloping up next. Clad in
fringed buckskins and a wide-brimmed black hat, he rode up alongside the wagon master at the head of the train. As the theme music
rolled on, the black and white screen filled with the image of the lithe-
limbed, cleft-chinned, raven-haired Robert Horton as Flint
McCullugh.

The Scout.

Those were the cowboy boots *I* wanted to crawl into. That was the job *I* wanted. It was Flint McCullugh who always rode miles out in front of that long, ponderous caravan. Flint McCullugh, the ever-vigilant eyes and ears of the wagon train. Flint McCullugh, probing out ahead, checking out the trail, looking for Indians, scouting out water holes, scanning the shimmering skyline with young eyes made old and wise by the miles he had ridden and the things he had seen. He was the first to smell danger, dodge the arrows, hear the muted thunder of far-away buffalo herds, and taste the bite of distant blizzards riding on the prairie wind. It was up to him to spot potential hazards, discern lurking enemies, and pick out the best and safest trail for the train to follow.

It seemed every episode would find Seth Adams growling at the wizened, bearded little cook, Charlie Wooster, "Now where in heck has that McCullugh gotten to?" But it wouldn't be long before the scout would come galloping back, jaw set, eyes flashing with danger, bearing news of the mysterious Up Ahead. That whole rolling community of men, women, and children relied on McCullugh's experience, alert judgment, and unfailing sense of direction. It was a dangerous thing, after all, this business of uprooting from comfortable homes and picket-fenced yards, putting your worldly goods and precious family into a wagon and setting off across a vast, trackless continent. The immigrants in their wagons couldn't see all the dangers ahead. They couldn't imagine what threatened over the next rise. They didn't know where to find water for their barrels or grass for their livestock.

They had to rely on The Scout.

It's always the image of Flint McCullugh that swims into my mind as I think about the role of a man as provider for his family. Now, that wouldn't make much sense if you thought only of the traditional definition of "provider." In our culture, when we think of provision, we think of food on the table and a roof over our heads. Actually, the emphasis in provision is *vision*. The *pro* part of the word indicates "before" or "ahead of time." "Vision" obviously speaks of "sight" or "seeing." What does that formula yield?

"There is a land where a man, to live, must be a man. It is a land of granite and marble and porphyry and gold—and a man's strength must be as the strength of the primeval hills. It is a land of oaks and cedars and pines—and a man's mental grace must be as the grace of the untamed trees. It is a land of far-arched and unstained skies, where the wind sweeps free and untainted, and the atmosphere is the atmosphere of those places that remain as God made them—and a man's soul must be as the unstained skies, the unburdened wind and the untainted atmosphere. It is a land of wide mesas, of wild rolling pastures and broad, untilled valley meadows—and a man's freedom must be that freedom which is not bounded by the fences of a too weak and timid conventionalism.

"In this land every man is—by divine right—his own king; he is his own jury, his own counsel, his own judge, and—if it must be—his own executioner.... In this land a man, to live, must be a man."

HAROLD BELL WRIGHT
Early Twentieth-Century Novelist

Looking ahead. Giving direction. Anticipating needs. Defining the destination. Riding ahead of the wagon on scout duty.

What makes a man? First, foremost, and above all else, it is *vision.* A vision for something larger than himself. A vision of something out there ahead. A vision of a place to go. A cause to give oneself for. Call it a sense of destiny. Call it a hill to climb. A mountain to conquer. A continent to cross. A dream glimmering way out there on the horizon. Call it what you will, but at its heart, it's vision. A man must visualize ahead of time. Project. Think forward. Lift his eyes and chart the course ahead. Ask leading questions. Picture the future. Anticipate what the months and years may bring. A provisionary is one who lives at and beyond the horizons. This is the very essence of his leadership. This is the "king" in every man...always looking ahead, watching out for his people, providing direction and order.

The physical necessities of life are the simplest, easiest duties of the provisionary. A little food, a little shelter, and physical provision is a done deal. But that isn't *real* provision. Thinking that food, clothing, and shelter equal provision is like confusing sex with love. Yes, it's a rather significant part of the story, but it isn't the whole book.

As men we so often misplace our vision. We focus myopically on houses and cars and stock portfolios and bank accounts and piling up *stuff.* We imagine we find status and security in these things, when in fact there is no status or security if you don't have relationships. We go to the "provide" part of the provisionary and say, "If I have a financial plan, if I've tucked away some money for college, if I have a good life insurance policy, I'm being a good provider." We revert to the things we can see, when in fact it is the *unseen* world, the world of the spirit, the world of relationships, where we ought to be majoring in our provision. Matters of character, heart, spirit, integrity, justice, humility—the kinds of things that last. The character traits that outlive a man and leave, not a monument, but a legacy.

What confidence that kind of masculine leadership brings—to an organization, to a family, to a church!

One of the strongest impressions I had growing up in central Washington was experiencing the *presence* of a man who always seemed to know where he was going. Because Pastor O. H. Williams knew why he was there and what he was about, I felt an enveloping sense of security every time I stepped through the doors of our little church. If he was there, everything was going to be okay. Kingdoms could rise and fall…no problem. Even if an airplane crashed through the roof of the church on Sunday morning, and there was total chaos, he would know just what to do. He always seemed to be able to look way down the road to see what was coming. And when the time came to take action on something, you always knew Pastor Williams would be in the lead, instructing and encouraging in that warm, steady, competent voice of his. Whenever he was on vacation, a vague uneasiness rippled through the ranks. People felt skittish. Restive. Out of sync. But when O. H. was back on the platform, a palpable sense of relief washed through the building. We could face whatever with calm certainty. The man was back.

Too many guys squander their vision—and then wonder why they lose their families. It's the all too common downside to superficial definitions of "success"…and don't let anyone snow you, *nothing* makes up for the failure of a family. At the heart of a real man's vision is the health of his family. If you have a family *that's your job!* What would have happened to the wagon train if Flint McCullugh had become distracted with hunting buffalo out there on the plains? Or prospecting for gold. Or painting nature scenes. Or digging for dinosaur bones. His job was to keep his eyes and ears open. To stay alert. To bend all of his energy and experience and strength to the critical responsibility of getting that little band of pioneers safely through dangerous territory to their destination.

Picture your family bumping along in a wagon. Your wife. Your kids. They're all there, moving through the wide mysteries of life, rolling inevitably toward a destination in the hazy distance. *What is that destination? How will your wagon get there?* As they travel in their fragile vessel of wood and canvas, they are terribly exposed. Vulnerable to the elements. Vulnerable to nameless enemies. Vulnerable to discouragement, weariness, distraction, disorientation. They're moving, but where are they going? They're crossing a frontier, but what perils lie ahead? Even on a clear day, from where they sit they can't see more than a few miles ahead. Your wife has wonderful vision, and can scan the skyline if she needs to. But God has uniquely equipped her to see things *close-up*, the details of making that wagon a secure and comfortable refuge. Your kids are bright and intelligent, but hey, they're in new territory. They're on strange turf. They have no idea what they'll be facing over the next rise. They romp and play and cut-up alongside the wagon as it pitches along, without a thought for deadly hazards and cruel enemies.

They're all looking to you, The Scout. They're depending on you to set the course, to determine the direction, to set the pace. They're looking to you for advance warning of storms, flash floods, box canyons, bottomless swamps, and waterless valleys ahead.

The measure of a man is the spiritual and emotional health of his family. A real provider has a vision for a marriage that bonds deeply, for sons with character as strong as trees, and for daughters with confidence and deep inner beauty. Without that vision and leadership, a family struggles, gropes, and may lose its way.

In J. R. R. Tolkien's classic fantasy, *The Hobbit*, a band of dwarves and one little hobbit are seemingly lost beyond hope in a vast, vile forest called "Mirkwood." Against all counsel and warning, they had strayed from the path, looking for food, and now found themselves in deadly peril from hunger, thirst, and nests of giant, sinister spiders. The ancient forest is so dense that the sky above is virtually obliterated by towering branches and thick foliage. Half-blind in the perpetual dusk and bereft of any sense of direction, the dwarves send Bilbo the hobbit (because he is smallest) up the slimy branches of a massive old tree to look for an end to the forest or a landmark or anything that might give the little party some hope of finding their way.

Up and up he climbs, until the little fellow finally reaches the tip-top of the hoary old giant. Swaying on the thin uppermost limbs, Bilbo at last sticks his head out of the foliage. He finds himself dazzled by the brilliant blue sky and golden sunlight—and nearly intoxicated by the sweet fresh air above and beyond the dank and rotting forest.

There *is* fresh air up there you know. There is direction and wisdom and landmarks that will never change. A man *can* get the perspective he needs to lead a family…if he is willing to humble himself and seek it from the Lord God. Consider the counsel of James:

But if any of you lacks wisdom, let him ask of God, who gives to all men generously and without reproach, and it will be given to him (James 1:5).

Men, if your family is lost in the woods, maybe it's time for you to climb a tree. Maybe it's time for you to get your head above the limbs and leaves, take a deep breath of fresh air, and scan the purple hills in the distance. The provisionary must know the difference between the forest and the trees. He needs to be able to scale the heights from time to time, and, with God's help, see the horizon.

It's not that men are genetically far-sighted while women are near-sighted. It has more to do with the God-given tendency of a man to look up and out and discern objects in the hazy distance and the tendency of a woman to read the fine print of relationships. A woman is simply a better reader. She has better focus on people and situations near at hand. She can read right away what's happening in the spirit, in a tone of voice, in a fleeting facial expression. That's why she so often tugs at the man. He gets so far "out there" in his provision role that he fails to see things under his very nose! Women place more emphasis on details, and on security.

I can remember when my wife didn't want to move into the new house we'd planned for months and months to purchase. When it came right down to signing the papers, she pulled up short. She didn't want to spend the money it would take to make that little leap forward. She was more security conscious, considering our monthly budget, and I kept thinking of long-term implications: *Where do we want our kids to grow up?*

Provisionaries need to use their God-given capacity for distance vision to encourage and give hope and security to their families. When they cannot or will not, the people under their roofs suffer loss.

Normally a very funny lady, writer Erma Bombeck describes her own childhood that wasn't so funny. She talks about a dad who failed to focus, who evidently failed as a provisionary. Yes, he "provided" in the material sense, but apparently gave little or no attention to the most profound aspects of provision. He had very limited contact with his family and, as is obvious from her comments, remained a complete mystery to his little daughter.

One morning my father didn't get up and go to work. He went to the hospital and died the next day. I hadn't thought that much about him before. He was just someone who left and came home and seemed glad to see everyone. He opened the jar of pickles when no one else could. He was the only one in the house who wasn't afraid to go into the basement by himself. Whenever I played house, the mother doll had a lot to do. I never knew what to do with the daddy doll, so I had him say, "I'm going off to work now"; and I put him under the bed. The funeral was in our living room, and a lot of people came and brought all kinds of good food and cakes. We never had so much company before. I went to my room and felt under the bed for the daddy doll, and when I found him, I dusted him off and put him on my bed. He never did anything. I didn't know his leaving would hurt so much.[1]

That little girl felt a gaping hole in her soul. It was a pain and emptiness she could well remember even as a middle-aged woman. Her daddy may have *thought* he was providing for the family, but he had missed something significant.

Helen Keller, blind and deaf from infancy, was asked what she regarded as the worst of handicaps. The questioner asked, "Is there anything worse than blindness?" "Oh, yes!" she responded. "A person with sight and no vision."

A provisionary sits at his young daughter's bedside at night when the lights are out and wonders aloud, "What kind of woman, what kind of wife and mother could you be for God?" A provisionary sits by the coals of a campfire and listens to a boy's hopes and dreams and nods his head and says, "Those are good dreams. I'm with you a hundred percent, son." A provisionary sits with his wife over coffee in the morning and says, "Where are we headed, anyway? What are our goals? Where are we going as a couple...as a family?" A provisionary looks down the years and asks himself questions.

If our marriage were to go on just the way it's been going, what will it be like for us in five, ten, twenty years?

How can I build the self-esteem of my wife who spends enormous amounts of time "cleaning house" and changing diapers?

How can I help my eight-year-old girl learn to understand and control her emotions before the hormones start pumping through her body?

When will my little boy and I need to have our first talk about sex?

What kinds of things might my kids encounter in middle school—and how can I prepare them?

How can I manage my career goals so that I'm available to my high school children?

What will my children need in a dad when they're in college?

What kind of a husband will my wife need when she hits menopause? How can I help her through that passage?

What kind of traits will my kids and grandkids cherish in a grand-father?

A provisionary helps keep the larger issues before his family so they won't be overcome by temporary setbacks or the disorienting fog of daily circumstances. People with places to go need to see ahead. Clarity of vision is critical to accomplishment of goals. A man was made for reaching goals, climbing mountains, and seeing ahead.

I recall climbing energetically toward the summit of a magnificent pass in the Eagle Cap Wilderness. The late Supreme Court Justice William O. Douglas called this area in the northeast corner of Oregon "the most beautiful piece of real estate on the planet." Others, standing in awe of the pristine mountain glory, have dubbed it "little Switzerland."

Marking our goal that day as we hiked was a nameless granite spire we called "little El Capitan." The pace was healthy. Spirits were high. Our towering granite landmark was a long way off from the bottom of the Minam River canyon, but the distance was irrelevant. The clear day was glorious, and we made excellent time just anticipating the beautiful scene awaiting us at Big Minam Meadows. On a clear day, as the song goes, you can see forever—and feel as if you could climb there, too. Everyone was caught up in the spirit of it.

And then…the weather closed in around us. The clouds dropped down into the tree tops. It began to drizzle. Our granite landmark disappeared, along with the horizon. Inevitably, our eyes dropped from the distant peaks to the top of our own boots. And we slowed. Boy, did we slow. The spring in our steps became pains in our legs. When you lose sight of your goal, you lose a lot more than that. Little things began to get to us. Someone has said, "We are slowed more by the grain of sand in our shoe than the mountain we climb." So true. The grain may have been there all along, but suddenly it takes on boulder proportions. Nothing was right anymore. *Whose idea was it to hike back into this forsaken wilderness, anyway?* The day seemed colder. Our pains seemed magnified. And the complaining set in. Irritability became the order of the moment.

What happened? How did glory turn into misery? The answer is simple enough: We lost our vision. We lost perspective. We were no longer drawing energy and gladness from that shining goal on the far horizon. Max Lucado capsulizes that transformation:

> Pilgrims with no vision of the promised land become propri-etors of their own land.... Instead of looking upward at [the Lord], they look inward at themselves and outward at each other. The result? Cabin fever. Quarreling families. Restless leaders. Fence building. Staked-off territory. No trespassing! signs are hung on hearts and homes. Spats turn into fights as myopic groups turn to glare at each other's weaknesses instead of turning to worship their common Strength.[2]

A man was made for vision. A husband was made for leading the way. A dad was made for vision-casting. Men, when was the last time you developed a five-year plan for your family? Have you dreamed it yourself? Shared it with your wife? Refined it together? Communicated it to the kids? Are they catching the spirit of the summit?

Say what you will about the Kennedy clan of Massachusetts, but the patriarch, Joseph P. Kennedy, did manage to cast a vision. As dis-torted as it may have been in the development of moral character, the vision was caught by several of his sons. Yes, there was ample money and privilege in the family, but it takes a lot more than money and privilege to develop in one family soldiers, senators, an attorney general, and a president of the United States. Behind it all, there was a dad with a vision; a dad who focused on the summit and drew several impressionable boys to follow his gaze.

In his own way, my father helped me begin scanning the horizon when I was just a little boy. If I saw a lot of little bitty print on the pages of the Bible, Dad saw mountain tops. When he prayed out loud, he always thanked God for "so great salvation" and for His glorious "Plan of the Ages." Now I didn't have an inkling what the Plan of the Ages was all about, but I didn't doubt that there was one, that it came from the heart of God,...and that it was glorious. It made me stand on my tip-toes to peer a little farther and deeper into spiritual mysteries. It brought security to my heart to realize what kind of a God I had, this great heavenly Planner who could look down the long ages and bring things to pass.

When you've lost your vision for who you are and where you are and why you-are-where-you-are, you find yourself powerless to take necessary action. Many of us have been so lulled to sleep by near-sighted images of life that we've forgotten we're in the midst of a great, cosmic battle. And because we can't see beyond our own tent flaps, our families are also stalled in camp, frustrated at every turn by an unseen enemy.

The king in Old Testament Scripture was the provisionary for his nation, and the champion of his people. That's the role God intended for Israel's first king, Saul. But somewhere in the early days of his tragic reign, Saul lost that vision. In one of the most familiar portions of Scripture, we find the whole fighting force of Israel stalled and languishing within shouting distance of their deadly enemies, the armies of Philistia. Because of Saul's unwillingness to face Goliath, the Philistine champion, and live out his God-given role, the Lord's army was stuck in camp, trembling in their tents. It finally took a clear-eyed teenager, fresh from the wide wilderness and the presence of God, to stand in the place of the provisionary and declare, "Who *is this* uncircumcised Philistine that he should taunt the armies of the living God?"

David looked around him with disbelief. "Hey! Look at what's going on around here!" he was saying. "Is everybody blind? This isn't right! Who is this lumbering ox to defy the armies of Yahweh? Don't you guys know who you are? You are *Israel* and this idol-worshiping Philistine is trying to stand in your way!" So David stepped in and took the initiative. He extracted Goliath like a bloody tooth and guess what? The troops woke up. And remembered their duty. And remembered their training. And remembered their mighty God. With a roar they charged across the valley to engage their enemy. That's what made the son of Jesse king, because kings are provisionaries.

How is it in your household? Does your family share a vision of a mountain-sized goal in the distance, flashing and glistening above the fog of disappointments and daily pressures? Is your wagon rolling toward a lush green valley on the other side of the continent? Is your vision wide enough and high enough and fine enough to keep the old wheels rolling through the dusty, sometimes monotonous plains of this adventure called life?

When you think about it, you don't have much time to step up to your high calling as wagon master and scout. The trek that seems so long now will soon be a memory. But there's time enough. Time enough to take that first step. Time enough to push your way through peripheral issues and life-draining preoccupations and ride out ahead of the family God has given you. Ready to saddle up? Then tighten the cinch and let's move out.

Wagons, *ho-oh!*

A Man Faces Himself

1. Who in your personal acquaintance seems to have the best handle on this issue of "vision"? Watch him carefully for the next few weeks. Jot down your observations of how he expresses his vision. Then take him to lunch, discuss with him your observations, and enjoy the movement in your own life.

2. Read through the questions on pages 28 and 29 of this chapter and answer each one for yourself.

3. Plan an evening away from the kids and other responsibilities. This one is just for you and your wife. Talk together about: (A) Your ideal "destination" for your family; (B) Where you think your family members might actually be in their personal journeys toward the destination; (C) How the two of you might work more deliberately together to get to where you want to be.

A Man Meets with His Friends

1. Is the role of "The Scout" natural or unnatural to you? Explain your answer.

2. In what specific ways do you find yourself "looking ahead" for your family? How do you "give direction"? If you asked each of the members of your family to describe the "destination" you have defined for them, what would they say?

3. Does our pro-vision major in the "stuff" of the seen world or the crucial issues of the unseen world? Knock this one around a bit until you begin to get a handle on it.

4. Have you ever known a man like Pastor O. H. Williams? If so, what kind of impression did he make on you?

5. Have you ever known a "person with sight and no vision"? If so, what impression did he make on you?

6. What do you think—is *your* vision "wide enough and high enough and fine enough to keep the old wheels rolling through the dusty, sometimes monotonous plains of this adventure called life?" Discuss this one at length with you friends. Draw courage and examples from one another.

The Four Pillars of Manhood:

A Man and His Roots

Four Mighty Ones are in every Man; a Perfect Unity
Cannot Exist but from the Universal Brotherhood of Eden,
The Universal Man...
WILLIAM BLAKE, "THE FOUR ZOAS"

ONCE UPON A TIME in the 1990s, several men went on a journey. Each man headed in the right direction. Each had the same destination burning in his heart. Each travelled long, weary miles in pursuit of a worthy goal. In time, each thought he had at last "arrived." Yet each fell tragically short of the objective. They journeyed far...but not one of them went far enough.

Several leading spokesmen of our nation's growing "men's movement" went looking for a definition of manhood. Each rightly realized that tepid water samples from the contemporary stream of manhood were hopelessly diluted and polluted. What each of them longed for was a long drink from the icy headwaters of masculinity.

Backtracking the stream through time, they sensed through some inner compass that they were walking in the right direction. They quickly splashed through the murky shallows of the nineties, eighties, and seventies. They hurried around the dark turbulence of the sixties and refused to linger at the compelling but deceptive currents of the fifties and forties. They went back. *Way back.* They traced the stream through ancient tributaries of legend, myth, and tribal lore.

The waters grew wilder and sweeter. The men listened for the throb of aboriginal drums, gazed at drawings etched on the walls of caves, and gathered snatches of songs and tales and myths that slept in mysterious pools and forgotten eddies.

And then there came a time when each explorer halted in his journey. One came to a place where the water seemed to pour from the naked rock. Another cleared the leaves away from a primeval spring. A third saw a torrent rippling down from a granite shelf. *Behold,* each said to himself, *the headwaters of Man.*

Each man stopped. Each man pitched his tent. Each man wrote his book.

But they fell short. They were headed in the right direction, but they stopped too soon.

For what they had imagined were headwaters were nothing of the sort. What they hoped were pure streams were already polluted. As close as they may have been, what they counted on as accurate depictions of True Masculinity were already warped and distorted. For behind every tributary, underground stream, and every bubbling creek, is the mother spring. The Genesis Spring. And if a man plunges his head into the cold artesian waters of *that* spring, so newly gushing from the very mind of God, he will taste something contemporary man and his well-meaning chroniclers know little of.

The taste of Original Man. Undiluted. Untainted.

So What Is Man? And Where Do You Go to Find Out?

Sam Keen, author of the best-selling men's book, *Fire in the Belly,* says he based his research on two sources. "The first source is my half-century-long study of the life of one man—myself.... The second source of my knowledge is from longtime friendships with a few men."

I appreciate Sam's honesty. But I choose not to define my manhood by either Sam's life or Sam's friends. In my opinion, he's still caught in the dark currents of the sixties and the murky backwaters of the seventies.

Robert Bly, author of the landmark, *Iron John*, wisely travels much further back in time to what he calls "the old stories":

The knowledge of how to build a nest in a bare tree, how to fly to the wintering place, how to perform the mating dance—all of this information is stored in the reservoirs of the bird's instinctual brain. But human beings, sensing how much flexibility they might need in meeting new situations, decided to store this sort of knowledge outside the instinctual system; they stored it in stories. Stories, then—fairy stories, legends, myths, hearth stories—amount to a reservoir where we keep new ways of responding that we can adopt when the conventional and current ways run out.[1]

But some things never change. Like the nature of man, for example. Or the nature of *a* man. Nevertheless, Bly is on to something here. There is something foundational and solid in the old stories. And the older the stories, the more foundational their truth.

But where does one go for the Story of Stories? Where else but to the Book of Books!

In my family room sits a brand new stereo system. The last one, purchased years ago, died a natural death. The new one arrived last week. Umpteen pounds of boxes, cases, wires, and manuals. *Manuals!* It took some careful reading, some sweaty wrestling, and not a little frustration, but my youngest son and I patched it together.

My friend, Moishe Rosen, says it well: "You get a microwave [or a stereo], you get a book. You get a toaster, you get a book. You get a car, you get a book. You get a life, you get a Book." Stands to reason. The patent holder issues the owner's manual. Born a human—male or female—you get a Book. Think of the Bible as the owner's manual for your masculinity. Think of it as the mother spring. The Headwaters. And drink deeply from it.

The point should be clear. We must not plant our manhood in the "mid-air" of current sexual politics. When we ask, "What is a man?", we're not going to query John Wayne or Gloria Allred. We're not going to ask Alan Alda, Archie Bunker, Dagwood, Tom Brokaw, Donald Trump, Mr. Mom, or Patricia Schroeder. We're going to ask the Creator what He had in mind when He invented the man.

We're going to get on our knees—not to crawl into some dank and odorous sweat lodge—but to humble ourselves before the Maker of men. Ironically, Sam Keen, on the very first page of his best seller, notes, "My grandmother gave me a Bible with a note that said: 'Read this every day, Big Boy—it will make you a real man.'" Good advice. Had it been followed, it would have saved Sam a lot of work. Not to mention a lot of grief.

So put on your thinking cap and tie on your running shoes. We're going to jog through some history and a little theology. It's back to the Bible, guys. I'm reminded of the ad campaign for the cereal giant Kellogg corporation. Seems the company flagship, the venerable Corn Flakes, was dropping in sales. The clever ad beckoned, "Kellogg's Corn Flakes...taste them again for the first time." In that spirit, let's you and I look at manhood from God's perspective. Sure, it's been there a long time. But if it's all starting to look like a bowl of soggy corn flakes, maybe we need to taste it again...for the first time.

Four Pillars

North. South. East. West. Four points on the compass.

Spring. Summer. Fall. Winter. Four seasons in the year.

Earth. Wind. Fire. Water. Four elements on the planet.

King. Warrior. Mentor. Friend. Four rhythms in a man.

Four undergirding life rhythms throb in the veins of every male-child. They pipe a four-part cadence to which every man must march if he chooses to be a complete man. Always intermingled, never exclusive, they provide the primary colors of the masculine rainbow from which all others draw their hue. Blending perfectly with one another, they reflect the light of the One in whose image they are made.

To the degree they are balanced, the image is clear and the man and those around him flourish. To the degree they are abased and abused, the image is distorted, the man withers, and those around him experience pain.

I like to call these qualities the four unshakable pillars of masculinity. These pillars are visible in both the sacred Scriptures of God,

"This was not a great year for guys.... Guys are in trouble. Manhood, once an opportunity for achievement, now seems like a problem to be overcome. Plato, St. Francis, Leonardo da Vinci, Vince Lombardi—you don't find guys of that caliber today. What you find is terrible gender anxiety, guys trying to be Mr. Right, the man who can bake a cherry pie, go shoot skeet, come back, toss a salad, converse easily about intimate matters, cry if need be, laugh, hug, be vulnerable, perform passionately that night and the next day go off and lift them bales onto that barge and tote it. Being perfect is a terrible way to spend your life, and guys are not equipped for it anyway. It is like a bear riding a bicycle: He can be trained to do it for short periods, but he would rather be in the woods doing what bears do there."

Humorist
GARRISON KEILLOR
in an op-ed piece in
the *Sunday New York Times*

and the secular history of man. But whether one studies the Creator or His creature, the truth is one. The Bible is filled with references, both explicit and implicit, to all four pillars. All four are both divine and human. In man, they are sometimes unbalanced and abusive. In Christ, they majestically merge in the ultimate Man.

You can see the pillars all across human history. For a secular vision of these same four foundational elements see *King, Warrior, Magician, Lover*, the insightful book by Robert Moore and Douglas Gillette. The authors write:

> It is our experience that deep within every man are blueprints, what we can also call 'hard wiring,' for the calm and positive mature masculine...instinctual patterns and energy configurations probably inherited genetically throughout the generations of our species. These archetypes provide the very foundations of our behaviors—our thinking, our feeling, and our characteristic human reactions. They are the image makers that artists and poets and religious prophets are close to.[2]

What Moore and Gillette call "blueprints" I prefer to see as fingerprints, the tell-tale mark of the Artist on the original.

A Closer Look at the Four Pillars

Let's walk closer to those majestic pillars. They're tall. They cast long shadows across a desolate landscape. Maybe if we get the right lighting, we'll be able to read the inscriptions.

King

THE KING function is clearly central to Scripture's themes. Our God is the King of kings. His Son, the second Adam, is destined to rule "with all power and authority." Adam, the prototype man, is instructed beside the Genesis Spring to "have dominion."

THE HEART OF THE KING is a provisionary heart. The king looks ahead, watches over, and provides order, mercy, and justice. He is authority. He is leader. He is Flint McCullugh and Seth Adams on one horse and under one hat. He is, in Moore and Gillette's words, "the energy of just and creative ordering." The king in a man is "under orders" from higher Authority.

Warrior

THE WARRIOR function is equally unmistakable in Scripture. Our God is the Warrior of both Testaments. Gentle Jesus, meek and mild? He closes the Book on a white war horse, in a blood-spattered robe, with a sword in His mouth and a rod of iron in His hand. The Book ends with a roar, not a whimper. Within the epistles, the mature believing man is often described in militant terms—a warrior equipped to battle mighty enemies and shatter satanic strongholds.

THE HEART OF THE WARRIOR is a protective heart. The warrior shields, defends, stands between, and guards. According to Moore and Gillette, he invests himself in "the energy of self-disciplined, aggressive action." By warrior I do not mean one who loves war or draws sadistic pleasure from fighting or bloodshed. There is a difference between a warrior and a brute. A warrior is a protector. Whether he's stepping on intruding bugs or checking out the sounds that go "bump" in the night. Whether he's confronting a habitually abusive Little League coach or shining a flashlight into a spooky basement. Whether he is shoveling snow or helping women and children into the last life boat on the Titanic. Men stand tallest when they are protecting and defending.

A warrior is one who possesses high moral standards, and holds to high principles. He is willing to *live* by them, *stand* for them, *spend himself* in them, and if necessary *die* for them. No warrior ever made that more obvious than Jesus of Nazareth. He who is the Ultimate PeaceMaker will establish that peace from the back of a great white horse as the Head of the armies of heaven.

Maybe these are some of the reasons why the most humiliating thing you can call a man is "coward." And maybe—just maybe—the warrior in a man explains something else about him. Ever notice how aloof a man can appear at times? Could it be that the warrior in him is a little out of sync? Soldiering, after all, is connected with pain. And pain hurts. A warrior gets accustomed to strapping on layers of protective insulation. Even a tender heart can be effectively hidden under a half inch of armor-plate.

When you're made to be a protector and soldier, it can be hard to display that tender side. Every parent of a little boy knows that warrior tendencies are part of the package. They arrived when the boy did. It doesn't matter if you never give your little guy a toy gun; he'll use his finger. Appalled at the idea of a toy hand grenade? Creative little warriors get by fine with exploding dirt clods, nuclear pine cones, or high-concussion snow balls. I heard from one frustrated lady on this score just a few weeks ago. She didn't want her little boy to conform to such violent societal expectations. She wanted him to play with *peaceful* things. Imagine her chagrin when he came roaring out of the bedroom squeezing off round after round from the protruding leg of a fuzzy teddy bear.

Why did he do that? It's just part of who he is as an apprentice defender.

Mentor

THE MENTOR function is not only modeled through the pages of the Bible, it is explicitly *commanded* in the form of "teaching them to observe" and "discipling." Our God is the Teacher in whose instruction we "delight." The only Perfect Man was the Discipler of all nations. And men who follow Him are to "teach others also."

THE HEART OF THE MENTOR is a teaching heart. The mentor knows. He wants others to know. He models, explains, and trains. He disciples—first his wife and kids, then others. He has a spiritual heart. As Moore and Gillette note (in the archetype they refer to as the "magician"), he exercises "the energy of initiation and transformation."

A man is supposed to *know* things. Like how a car runs. Or the inner workings of a hair dryer. Or the capitol of Nepal. Or how many legs are on a spider. Or how many miles to the next rest stop. Or when the weather will turn. It's up to him to maintain a working knowledge of why electricity flows, dogs bark, birds migrate, hamsters die, trees lose their leaves, dads lose their hair, and girls down the street "act weird."

Why do family members ask the man of the house these things? Because men are supposed to know how things work. And what to do next. And where to go from wherever you are. Men are supposed to be able to teach life.

Friend

THE FRIEND (or "lover"—but never to be prostituted by the isolated erotic) is the function most endearing. We are drawn to God who defines Himself by it: "God IS love." He insists that the ultimate point of all Scripture centers on loving Him and one another. It is at one and the same time the most basic instruction of Scripture and the "new commandment" given to every man.

THE HEART OF THE FRIEND is a loving heart. It is a care-giving heart. Passionate, yes. But more. Compassionate ("I will be with you"). The friend in a man is a commitment-maker. And a promise-keeper. His is "the energy that connects men to others and to the world" (Moore and Gillette). More on friendship to come in later chapters.

Sourced in Scripture, observed in history, and experienced personally, these four pillars bear the weight of authentic masculinity. They co-exist. They overlap. And when they come together in a man, you will know it. You will feel it. You will be touched by it. Like four strands of steel in a cable, they will hold you.

I will never forget a lonely night in my life when that steel cable kept me from falling into darkness.

The Touch of a Four-Pillared Man

I was a freshman in college. It was winter on the Chicagoland campus of Wheaton College. Late winter. Cold, wind-blown, drifting snow, dead winter. A lot like my soul right then—lifeless. A combination of things had thrown me into a tailspin. It was my first time away from home for an extended season. Away from the girlfriend who would someday become my wife. I'd been disappointed by the winter sports season. I was fighting the fierce deadlines of academia. But worst of all—and for the first time in my rather sheltered life—I found myself reeling from the intellectual loss of my faith.

Never in my life had I felt so disoriented. So alone. I couldn't sleep. Couldn't study. Couldn't speak with anyone. I could only walk, kick rocks, and commiserate with the silent, frozen landscape. That's what I was doing about midnight.

I stumbled aimlessly across the deserted center of campus, lost in myself—a terrible place to be. Then, out of nowhere, I was touched by a Tender Warrior. Literally. Without any inkling whatsoever that there was anyone else alive out there, I felt a hand on my shoulder.

A voice fought its way through the wind. "Could I be helpful to you?"

I looked up into the face of Dr. Hudson Armerding, the great-hearted president of Wheaton College.

Apparently he had stayed late in the office that night. I still don't know how he found me. Had he seen me wandering in the darkness? Had he felt my pain and desolation from a second-floor window? I don't know how he got there, but there he was—at my side—a four-sided tower of strength. The king in him bore the weight of the college on his shoulders. The warrior in him fought powerfully through the blood-draining battles facing any college president of the sixties. The mentor in him taught us history in class, the Scriptures in chapel, and life in general. And the friend in him reached out and drew in a hapless freshman wandering in a deep, months-long funk.

He invited me to his home. We walked the distance together. There in the warmth of his living room, with everyone else in the house long asleep, he fixed two cups of tea. We talked. And talked. He became my friend. He still is. One of a half dozen men who have marked my life, Hudson Armerding will always be a consummate King-Warrior-Mentor-Friend to me.

The four pillars of masculinity were balanced in Dr. Armerding. Like four strands of steel, they were woven together to form a cable that is the spine of masculinity. A "good man" is the balance of the four. A good warrior is also a sensitive lover. A Tender Warrior. A good friend is always a helpful mentor. The four are inseparable in a good man. In balance, they are every man's purpose, every woman's dream, and every child's hope. Abused, they are the curse of every man, woman, and child.

Masculinity Means Initiation

Taken together, the four steel strands form the single cable-like spine for masculinity. Taken together, they may be described in a single word. The one word that marks a man. The overarching element in masculinity. Coloring each of the four pillars, it is distinct from them. Call it initiative. Masculinity means *initiation*.

Among the ancient Hebrew words for man is one meaning "piercer." Its feminine counterpart is "pierced one." While the anatomical or sexual elements are clear, the force of the words is much larger in scope. The physical is a parable of the spiritual. The visible is a metaphor for the invisible. The tangible speaks for the intangible. At his core a man is an initiator—a piercer, one who penetrates, moves forward, advances toward the horizon, leads. At the core of masculinity is initiation—the provision of direction, security, stability, and connection.

Ever been to a function where there was no one to take the initiative? Recently on the news I watched a curious scene. A throng of people had gathered outside a doorway on a downtown sidewalk. It was to be the opening day of classes at a local professional school. But no one from the school staff showed up. No faculty. No administration. No leadership. No initiative.

The would-be students, without direction, milled around like hapless cattle. No one knew what to do. No one even knew quite what to think, say, or feel. There was only chaos. Tempers flared, but no initiation. There were sighs and groans and curses, but no direction. As it turned out, the school officials had simply closed the place without notice and never bothered to show up to say so. The result was sheer anarchy, complete confusion, and total disorientation all rolled into one scene.

Ever seen an orchestra without a conductor? A team without a quarterback? A boat with no rudder? A compass without a needle? Pretty pathetic. Nothing works right. Ever seen a man without initiative? Like a compass without a needle is not a compass, a man without initiative is not a man.

Masculinity means initiation. To be masculine is to take initiative. To provide direction, security, stability, and order. To lead. To head. To husband. Masculinity means initiation. (Nowhere does it mean "bossy"—more on that later.)

A Four-Pillared Man Takes Initiative

I have a friend who epitomizes initiative. Like a lot of us, he came to a place in life where it just wasn't all it was cracked up to be. Too workaday. Oh, he was climbing the ladder. He was clearly the CEO's "fair haired boy"—with a bright future by most people's standards. But not by his own. There were too many deadlines that belonged to someone else. Too many weekends in faraway hotel rooms. Too many late evenings in the office. And not enough time with those he loved most—his family.

A lot of guys feel that way. A lot of people pass through life feeling trapped in some vague sense of dissatisfaction. Some advance beyond the trapped feeling to nurse a dream in their hearts. But not very many do something about it. After all, we rationalize, I have to pay the bills. I'm kind of stuck. No time to look around. No money to launch out. No energy to spend for myself. It's too bad I can't be around to see the kids grow up…but I'll just have to hang on, tough it out, and retire someday. Maybe then I'll have some time. But not now.

Not my friend. He decided to do something about it. He took the initiative. He put some feet to the dream and some plans on paper.

The day came when he walked into the CEO's office and resigned. His dream of starting his own company required too much capital to do it immediately. So he leased the necessities. Rented the facilities. Borrowed some know-how from those already doing it. And worked hard. It grew. He found a silent partner. The endeavor grew some more. And in just a few short years, as the two of us and our wives spent an evening together, he smiled and said, "Today was the day. We incorporated. We have our own company."

It's still growing. And he's doing it all over again in another field. Initiative. Doing something about it.

My friend was looking ahead for the family. Peering into the distance at storms on the horizon. Providing like a king. He was also protecting his family from the encroaching dangers of busyness. Protecting like a warrior. He was dogged in his determination to model for his kids by saying no to the ever increasing demands of being a "company man." Mentoring by example. And he was resolute in procuring a lifestyle that fostered loving friendship within that little band of folks under his own roof.

Initiation is the bottom line of masculinity. It means taking the lead. The lead in providing, protecting, mentoring, and befriending. It means caring for and developing our mates, our children, and ourselves. It means taking the lead in apologizing. The lead in seeking forgiveness. The lead in vulnerability. Masculinity means initiation. C. S. Lewis, as you might expect, said it brilliantly: "God is so masculine, that all of creation is feminine by comparison."

Expanding on that thought, Elisabeth Elliott writes:

The earth has always been seen in the human imagination as female. Mother Earth. Mother Nature. The sun is usually thought of as male, often as a god. For the earth receives, is acted upon and gives back in fertility what is planted, while the sun receives nothing from the earth, but shines in his strength upon her, giving her life. Here we have the ancient and deep human consciousness of maleness and femaleness.[3]

Taste It Again

Taste it again for the first time. All four masculine archetypes are observable in the headwaters of Eden. They flow from the Genesis Spring, in both the words and the white spaces, to touch all of Scripture. Adam was to have dominion, to provide order and supervision for the garden, to look-out for it. He was to protect his helpmate, to stand between her and the Evil there. The warrior in Adam must have been on leave when the enemy invaded the garden. Adam was to teach his wife what God had taught him. It is evident the Creator had intended that Adam pass on to his wife the instructions he had received—something he apparently failed to do well inasmuch as she was the more easily deceived. And Adam was to cleave to his wife in the most intimate of friendships.

Unfortunately, the king and warrior qualities of manhood are suspect today. Of the four pillars, they are the most tarnished and eroded in our culture. Few object to a man being a mentor or a friend. Many resist the king and the warrior. Authority and strength seem to be questionable virtues in our day. But we miss them in this turbulent, rootless culture of ours. Oh, how we miss them! Without them, we are hollow men. We are men without chests.

A cable of four strands will bear an unbelievable load. Each strand lends strength to the others. Each quality weaves in balance and stability and endurance. There are plenty of weak ropes in our world today—cables that fray under pressure and snap in the storms. Let's be the kind of men that others can hang onto when skies get dark and life gets crazy.

Let's be the kind of cable that holds. The kind of cable that stays and stays and stays.

In the next chapter, we'll see just how much weight a cable like that can hold.

A Man Faces Himself

1. Match each of the "four pillars" mentioned in this chapter with a favorite Bible verse or character who especially captures that trait. Then ask a close friend, probably your closest, to place you in the category that most characterizes you. Talk about it.

2. Identify one area in which it is hard for you to take initiative (e.g., giving compliments, showing affection, family prayer, etc.) and plan for two or three specific times this week to take the initiative with it.

A Man Meets with His Friends

1. What figures defined "manliness" for you while you were growing up? How did these authorities define it?

2. What is the problem with defining "manhood" by the opinions of contemporary "experts"?

3. What is the advantage of defining "manhood" by biblical standards?

4. In what concrete ways do you live out your role as "king"?

5. In what concrete ways do you live out your role as "warrior"?

6. In what concrete ways do you live out your role as "mentor"?

7. In what concrete ways do you live out your role as "friend"?

8. Which of the four main roles is easiest for you? Which is most difficult? Why?

9. How is "taking initiative" different from "bossing around"?

10. In what areas do you easily take initiative? In what areas do you struggle with taking initiative?

Staying Power:

A Man's Greatest Strength

Never will I leave you;
never will I forsake you.
JESUS CHRIST, CENTURY 1

JUST A FEW TIMES in your life, you meet a man who stops you in your tracks. His presence fills a room. Charismatic but substantive. Confident but humble. Authoritative but gracious. Exuding strength but inviting companionship. He seems to have spent a lifetime at the headwaters. Drunk deeply from the sources of masculinity.

The more you learn of him, the more there seems to be. His character calls you to follow him. His success speaks well of him. His family reflects the quality of his leadership. This is the kind of guy you want to have breakfast with. Take fishing. Get to know. Learn from. Emulate.

This is a man who is just that. *A man.*

Years ago I had the privilege of meeting such a man. A landholder, rancher, and community leader, he was the most respected and influential individual in the entire region. But his greatest interest was his large, active family. In spite of enormous demands, there was always time for that tribe of his. His children were never an interruption. In fact, any conversation with him eventually included references to the kids. He realized that despite his enormous wealth, the only real legacy of any importance he would leave this world would be his sons and daughters. And he had an unusually well developed sense of spiritual things. He seemed to own a vision much larger than himself. He had a sense for eternity. This guy had it all. The blessings every man desires were all his—wealth, honor, family, health. And underneath it all, like bedrock, a sterling character.

His name was Job.

I met him in the oldest pages of Scripture in a book that bears his name:

> There was a man in the land of Uz, whose name was Job, and that man was blameless, upright, fearing God, and turning away from evil. And seven sons and three daughters were born to him. His possessions also were 7,000 sheep, 3,000 camels, 500 yoke of oxen, 500 female donkeys, and very many servants; and that man was the greatest of all the men of the east. And his sons used to go and hold a feast in the house of each one on his day, and they would send and invite their three sisters to eat and drink with them (Job 1:1-4).

It was a tradition. They were a close-knit outfit. On every birthday, the gang celebrated together. They belonged to each other, and the anchor in the middle was Dad.

> And it came about, when the days of feasting had completed their cycle, that Job would send and consecrate them, rising up early in the morning and offering burnt offerings according to the number of them all; for Job said, "Perhaps my sons have sinned and cursed God in their hearts." Thus Job did continually (Job 1:5).

The man from Uz carried his family in his heart. Even when the children had become adults, he carried them. Deep in his soul. And through his days, down through the years, he prayed for them, thinking, *The kids seem to be doing all right, but...maybe I'm missing something. Everything looks okay on the outside, but only God sees the heart. Who knows? Maybe one of them is teetering on the edge. Maybe one of them is facing a difficult choice today that would lead him away from God's plan.*

Job did this *continually*. The man's life was marked by his commitment to his family. In this, the oldest book of the Book, we get a look at a man who could still wet his beard near the ancient headwaters of masculinity. The kingly blood of Original Man still coursed through his veins.

Job was a Provisionary. And even though he was likely very generous, that "pro-vision" went far beyond material goods. By daily praying for his grown children and carrying them in his heart, he was always looking ahead. Always squinting toward the horizon, looking down the trail, scouting out potential dangers and hazards.

The story goes on (v. 8). Somewhere in the heavenlies, the Lord Himself is holding court. He is speaking to Satan, the great adversary of all men and families. This man, Job, occupies their conversation. The Lord says, "Have you considered my servant Job? For there is no one like him on the earth, a blameless and upright man, fearing God, and turning away from evil."

Satan shrugs. He replies, in effect, "Sure, he's one of Your good guys. Of course he is tight with You. He's got all the advantages. Who wouldn't be? You handle him with kid gloves. But just try taking a few of his precious toys, and *then* see how the tale reads."

You know the story from there. For reasons beyond our comprehension, Satan is given some freedom to do what he relishes most: destroy a man's life. He's on a leash, of course; he can go only so far. But for a brief season he is authorized to lay a dark hand on this good man's life. Given opportunity, he turns all his ugliness on Job.

In a series of life-blasting catastrophes, Job loses his business, his wealth, his health, and *all ten* of his dearly-loved children. At the peak of his agony, his wife mocks and lashes out at him. His friends jeer and accuse him. And heaven suddenly falls silent. The God whom Job so faithfully serves seems away from His desk. Job's urgent calls and cries are routed into cosmic voice mail. The worthy rancher from the land of Uz suddenly finds himself as alone as a man can be.

The question before the reader, the Lord, the Devil, and the ages is a strong one. Will Job remain a man, a real man? Will he wilt? Will he fall apart? Will he cut and run? Will he cash in the one thing he has left—his character, the essence of the man?

Some things can be taken away. Some cannot. I recall my first extended time away from home. It was my freshmen year in college. Having never before been east of Idaho, I now faced the prospect of an entire semester in a strange land called "Illinois." It might as well have been Siberia. Or Mars. It felt like forever. For a youngster accustomed to the mountains of the West, it seemed as though Illinois had no horizons. The gray, flat land and the dreary days seemed to drone on into eternity. I wanted nothing more than to come home. I dreamed of it. Longed for it. Framed a thousand valid reasons for bagging school and heading West. But for reasons I couldn't even articulate at the time, I stayed with it.

At last, after months of numbing endurance, I arrived in home country. As I stepped from the train, Dad emerged from the crowd and shook my hand. I'll never forget what he said.

"Son, you have something no one can ever take away from you. It's on the inside. You stuck it out. You've done some growing up."

He was right. People, events, evil schemes, disasters, catastrophes can take things away from you. Things on the outside. But no one can ever take away what's on the inside—heart, soul, character. A man can throw it away. But no one can ever take it away.

That was the question before Job. And that is the question before every man. When things around you are taken away, what will happen on the inside—where you live with yourself? Will character survive? Job proved his manhood. Out of his story comes what we have called for centuries "the patience of Job." I think that's selling it short. Job demonstrated something longer and stronger than patience. Shining out of his life through the dark horror of grief and loss is what I believe to be a man's greatest strength. His highest attribute. Call it patience if you like. I call it *staying power.*

What Is Staying Power?

In his letter to scattered and suffering Christians, James tagged that same quality "endurance." A literal rendering yields the phrase *staying under.* Remaining. Persevering. Holding fast. Standing firm.

That's what a man does. That's what a man is.

"The talk at the table turned to what women found interesting in men.... One girl said she liked a man with dark eyes.... Another girl said she preferred strong, muscular men. Another said she was attracted to men with beards. Then someone asked, 'Deirdre, what do you like in a man?' They fell silent waiting.

"She put her cloth to her mouth. The fire burned warmly at her back.

" 'It is good for a man to be strong,' she said. 'A strong man can do so many things. But a man who is both strong and gentle is wonderful. A man must be intelligent, of course, but if he is also humble, that makes him all the more appealing…a man who is strong enough to live a disciplined life, but who is tender with the faults of others…a man who is honest above all, but kind…a man with courage to stay with the same task year in and year out, even if it is boring or tiring or painful, simply because it is his duty…a man with the courage of faithfulness. I love all these things about a man.' There was…silence."

ROBIN HARDY
from *The Chataine's Guardian*

The military equivalent of "staying under" probably finds its ultimate fulfillment in an institution called army Ranger school. As a young army officer, I had been called on to endure unbelievably rigorous training before being shipped out to Southeast Asia. In the middle of my tour in Vietnam, I often wondered *How on earth could a guy survive this if he didn't have Ranger school?* The whole point of that training was to help us overcome our most basic fears, so that we could function no matter what kind of pressure or circumstances we would face in our future duties. The physical, mental, and emotional stress they put us under defies description. We went for days on end with little if any sleep. Stayed out for days on end with little if any food.

As I pen these words, I can picture our little company at four-thirty in the morning—what we called in the military "oh-dark-thirty"—crawling along on our bellies under logs and through mucky, water-filled trenches. Late afternoon would find us staggering with exhaustion and bleeding from the feet after forced marches of endless miles. And just when we thought we were going to expire some officer would be in our face screaming, "Drive on, Ranger, *drive on!*"

Through it all, we began to find out something about the limits of a man's mind and body. We *could* get along without food. We *could* function without sleep. We *could* go day after day after day after day—even on past the end of our frayed rope. They proved to us that we could do what we had to do.

Job would have done well in Ranger school. Because he exhibited an enormous staying power. Think of it. He was a man whose masculinity rested

—not in what he owned
—not in the size of his home
—not in the amount of his investments
—not in what he could perform
—not in what he could achieve
—not in people he knew
—not in what model of donkey he rode
—not in his status in the community.

Job proved himself quite apart from decorations and tributes and trophies and newspaper clippings. Job sourced his masculinity and personhood in who he was, alone and naked before God. And that makes a man out of you.

There was a sense of permanence in Job. He was strong, stable, secure, consistent throughout. What you saw was what you got—whether he had the visible trappings of God's blessing or not. In sickness and in health. For better or for worse. For richer or for poorer. *Job stayed.* Sounds like a marriage vow, doesn't it? For good reason. You see, that marriage covenant and the spirit of those words are at the core of a man's manhood. A man's greatest strength is his capacity to stay by the stuff. To make and keep promises. A man's word connects. A man's word stays.

At one point the old patriarch vows, "Though He slay me, yet will I trust Him." Standing tall in the fierce winds of hell itself, Job refuses to turn from his commitment. And that is masculinity, pure and unadulterated.

But Men Aren't Staying

It is this staying power that makes and marks a man. Not climbing ladders. Not grabbing for the gusto. Not frenzied movement. Certainly not leaving our wives. Not abandoning our families. Not disappearing into passivity. Today's real men are a vanishing breed, and it's killing our culture. The curse of our day is not so much the AIDS epidemic as it is men who don't know what a man is and who cut and run from their wives and families.

Have you noticed how badly men run in our culture?

• One-third of American children are not living with their natural fathers.
• Over fifteen million kids are growing up in homes without any father.
• Seventy percent of men in prison grew up without a father.

According to *Newsweek* (January 13, 1992), "Through most of the 1970s and 80s, a million children a year watched their parents split up."

Often when I read statistics like these, the names of men I have known personally come to mind. Some of those names and faces had been part of the church I pastor. But they are gone now. Gone from their wives, their children, their homes, and their church. I confess their names bring a measure of disrespect to my mind. I know they experienced pain. I know there was pressure. I know it wasn't easy. I know "there are two sides." But the bottom line is, they ran. They didn't stay. Didn't keep their word. "Till death do us part" was evidently a Hollywood line to them. They wanted to be men. They wanted to be strong and virile. But when they ran, what strength they lost!

They were looking for their virility, and in thinking they would find it somewhere else, they lost it. But it's still out there in front of them like some cruel mirage they'll never reach. For them it wasn't "women and children first." It was "me first." That's a little boy, not a man. In their frantic chase after "happiness" they lost their manhood, perhaps never to regain it.

The Painful Results of Running

Some time ago I received a letter from a young man in our church. He described what it was like for him in his pilgrimage toward manhood. My heart went out to him. With great pain he described his life during those tender, momentous years of middle school. Because of broken marriage vows, during those critical years he had four different "mothers," lived in three different states, attended six different schools, and "moved in and out of more houses than I literally can remember."

The legacy continues. His father was recently divorced for the sixth time. An older brother just separated from his second wife. Another older brother is divorced. A sister has been married twice. And his birth mother has married three times. He's determined it will be different when he marries. He wants to be a man. But it's a fearful thing for him because he knows that children of divorce never *fully* recover.

In the 1980s, divorce destroyed millions of homes and the people in them. In one year alone there were 1,155,000 divorces. In another sample year, of the 2,487,000 weddings performed, 25 percent involved a bride who had been married previously. Since 1920 the divorce rate in this country has increased 1,420 percent![1]

That's a lot of pain. The baby boomers are divorcing at a rate twice that of their parents. Pity the children. In our country more than a million kids a year experience the shock of marital breakup. Sociologist Andrew Cherlin of Johns Hopkins University says, "Today's children are the first generation in this country's history who think divorce and separation are a normal part of family life."[2]

Child psychologist, Dr. David Elkind writes:

We see more children who show symptoms of stress, headaches, stomach aches, low mood, learning problems. As they get older, many of them feel they've missed an important part of their life. They feel used and abused. My concern is if they don't feel cared about, then they can't ever care about anyone else, let alone themselves. We may be creating a large number of children who are emotional misfits.[3]

A personal friend of ours was a school teacher before she started her own family. Today her children are in the upper grades and she has returned to the classroom after a fourteen year hiatus from teaching. Recently my wife asked her, "Do you notice any obvious difference in the classroom now that you're back after those years?" Her response was unhesitating: "The emotional instability of the children!"

One study found that 42 percent of children of divorced parents hadn't seen their father for a year or longer.[4]

Our world is falling apart for lack of kings, warriors, mentors, and lovers. For lack of men who will stay. Who will keep their word. Despite the obstacles. Despite the opposition. Despite their pain.

Keeping Your Word Is Critical

The ability to make and keep promises is central to manhood. It may be trite to say that "a man's word is his bond" but it is never trite to see it in action. It is a man at his best—giving his word and making good on it, making a promise and keeping it. The calling of every man is to offer stability to a world full of chaos. Certainty to a jungle of unpredictability. Consistency to a world in flux. Security to an insecure place.

We live in a "hope so" world. There are few certainties in this life. Ours is a world of dreams, hopes, and wishful thinking. Everyone "hopes" their ship will come in. But we joke, a trifle uncomfortably, that only death and taxes are certain. We "hope"

—that our marriages will work out
—that we will find fulfillment
—that our children will turn out okay
—that we'll be able to keep a decent job.

Everyone would love to change their hope to certainty. And we can, in the things that matter. The things inside. A real man brings certainty to his world by the power of a promise.

Promise making and keeping is at the heart of godliness. At the heart of God—at the very core of His nature—is the making and keeping of promises. All the Scripture hangs on a promise—a series of covenants. A man's promise is an awesome power. Lewis Smedes said it well: "When a man makes a promise, he creates an island of certainty in a heaving ocean of uncertainty.... When you make a promise you have created a small sanctuary of trust within the jungle of unpredictability."[5]

When Grandpa Weber used to tell me, "You're a Weber boy," I knew exactly what he meant. It meant you told the truth, and you kept your word. Even though I was just a little chip when he said those words to me, they've echoed in my heart for my entire life. I wanted to live up to being a Weber boy...which meant, *Always, always keep your word. When you lose that, you've lost yourself.*

Linda and I married just over a quarter century ago, and we had not a twit of an inkling of what those twenty-five-plus years would bring. How could we possibly have imagined what the winds of the years would blow into our lives? War in Vietnam and agonizing separation. Financial pressure. Miscarriage. The stress of ministry. The pain of criticism. The weight of responsibility. And more. When we stood together at the altar that sunny afternoon, we couldn't have guessed a tenth of it.

But we didn't need to. We made a promise. We recited a vow.

Out of the whole world, we chose each other. And the power of that choice, that promise, has kept us. There is no question in either of our minds that we could find a "better mate." Does that surprise you? It shouldn't. There is always someone out there better than you. There will always be someone more beautiful, intelligent, wealthy, witty, competent, sensitive, or sensual. But that's a nonissue to Linda and me. The toxin of comparison has been utterly neutralized and washed away by the sacred anti-toxin of a promise.

Building a Secure Place

A man's greatest strength is his enormous staying power. Job stayed. He had intentions.

> I shall die in my nest,
> And I shall multiply my days as the sand.
> My root is spread out to the waters,
> And dew lies all night on my branch.
> My glory is ever new with me,
> And my bow is renewed in my hand
> (Job 29:18-20).

Weldon Hardenbrook says it well:

> The stability of Job's lifestyle stands in vivid contrast to the anxious mobility that permeates our society where almost 25 percent of the population moves each year.... It's extremely difficult for people to build [a] healthy identity when they are always on the move.... Some of the most problem-ridden families I work with are those who never stay put. They move on before they are able to become a stable part of the community, on to a new town, a new neighborhood, a new church.[6]

Maybe there are some implications there for us men. In a day when the thing to do seems to be climbing this ladder or that ladder (yes, usually to find them leaning on the wrong wall), maybe it would be good for a man to spend less time climbing and moving and more time staying and building.

Years ago, as a twenty-five-year-old Green Beret Captain in the Republic of Vietnam, experiencing that first wake-up call, I found myself with an increasing desire to invest my life in the things that mattered most to Christ. Linda and I made a decision to invest at least the next twenty-five years of our lives in the two institutions and organizations that God Himself gives primary attention to—the family and the local church. Our family and His family. It was a simple train of thought: Those are the two things He loves most. Those are the two most foundational organisms on earth in our day—organisms that are alive and reproductive and therefore leave legacies that far outlive our individual lives. It made sense that we would give the best years of our lives to these endeavors. That meant I needed to know more about Him and His Word. That meant school. I had already finished college, so seminary seemed the logical choice. I thought they "made monks" in seminary, but, hey, if that's what it took, I was willing.

I started seminary with one wife and two sons and finished with a third (son, that is). During those years a conviction began to set in: We really wanted the boys to grow up in one place, establish friends in one community, experience the same high school and its teams, and basically know where "home" was. Roots are critical to growing things, and families are built with staying power. But the life of a pastor had always seemed to be a fairly mobile one. So we prayed...and we stayed. Some choice "professional opportunities" have come and gone. We're still here. One town. One home. One school district. And one church. We all know where home is, and we all like that very much. Even though one son is in graduate school overseas, one is in college in the Midwest, and one in ministry, the roots are healthy.

King David of Israel, a man's man if there ever was one, said, "Lord, who can abide in your tent?" It's another way of asking, *What kind of man is a real man, the kind who could live like You, the Inventor of man? What kind of man lives well in Your eyes?* The answer to David's question reads, "He who walks with integrity...and speaks truth in his heart...he who swears to his own hurt, and does not change."

In other words, the kind of man who pleases God is a man of his word. One who makes and keeps promises. One who "swears to his own hurt." *One who stays.* That kind of man creates an atmosphere of stability in an ocean of insecurity.

Contemporary Models of Staying Power

Can you think of men like that in your past? An uncle, a teacher, a coach, a grandfather, a neighbor? Memories of men who stayed are like firm handholds in the long, sometimes slippery climb to the highlands of masculinity. My mind lingers on a bald, bespectacled, barrel-shaped gentleman who stayed and stayed and stayed. He was my pastor as I was growing up, and though he left for Home several years ago, his memory fills me to this day with warmth and courage. Every now and then I catch a glimpse of him up there in the grandstands, and it makes me walk a little straighter under my load and hang on a little tighter to my God-given responsibilities.

O. H. Williams was far more capable in gifting and vision than our little church in central Washington had the wits and wisdom to realize. He could have taught in most Bible colleges across the country. But he passionately believed in the ministry of the local church. He was a born shepherd, and he stayed at that task. Orville Williams would never have come to the Yakima Valley if he had been looking for "position." But a man perseveres in a task because he sees the forest and lives above the silly trees.

As a youngster, I watched with horror and disbelief as a determined faction of self-inflated, self-appointed "church guardians" in our congregation set out to destroy this good man's ministry. Not content to ridicule and criticize Pastor Williams himself, they also went after his family. They snipped away at his teenaged son and daughter. They roundly criticized his sweet wife, Sylvia. Not even their shy, five-year-old daughter escaped their poisoned arrows.

Years after Orville's death, Sylvia told our family she could always tell when he got one of "those calls" at night. Ask any pastor about "those calls"…those sharp, venomous, critical calls that come at night when you're tired and emotionally low and have poured yourself out doing your best. As the call would get longer and longer, Sylvia told us, Orville's voice would get softer and sweeter. That's how she knew the call was hurting him.

Eventually, that faction in the church ran the Williams family out of town on a rail. And of one of the finest preachers I've ever heard, they said he couldn't preach. Couldn't preach! That little crackerbox church deserved King Herod, yet God, in His inscrutable grace, had given them a Tender Warrior.

Years later, college had come and gone for me. Then came the military and the war. I sensed God's call while sweating through the horror of Vietnam, and after my discharge, enrolled in seminary.

But I had a problem.

I was committed to the Lord, committed to ministry, but I refused in my heart of hearts to ever be a pastor. It wasn't so much that *I* couldn't handle the criticism. I thought I could stand up to it. But I didn't want my wife to be a target for small-minded sharpshooters. I didn't want my children to be gaped at like guppies in a goldfish bowl.

I knew Orville was pastoring in Eugene, so I drove down Interstate 5 one Saturday afternoon and knocked on the Williams' door. Sylvia set us up in the living room with coffee and cookies and I opened up and told Pastor (he will always be my pastor) my struggle. I was committed to serving the Lord. But I just couldn't stomach the idea of the pastorate.

He looked at me for a moment as he cleaned his glasses with a white, folded hanky. "Stu," he said slowly, "are you saying what you're saying because of what you saw up in Washington? Because of what happened to us?"

"Of course," I said. I was just a teenager at the time, but I remembered the pain that the family went through. And I remembered him, politely and humbly exiting the scene because he thought it was time.

"I don't want *my* wife to go through that," I told him heatedly, "and I don't want my children to go through that. I don't want to be a piece of public property."

In a gesture that pastors the world over use when they're about to nail you, Orville tilted his head to one side and sat back in his chair.

"Well," he said quietly, "that's pretty much the whole point of the ministry."

"What?" I said, not sure I was hearing right.

"That's pretty much the whole point of the ministry. To be a piece of public property. You know, Stu, just last week another man sat in that very chair where you're sitting now. He's the regional manager for a large corporation. He told me, 'I'm tired of being a company man.

I'm tired of the way I'm being treated.'"

Pastor Williams' round face crinkled into a smile. "Criticism and stress and troubles aren't something exclusive to ministry, Stu. They're *life.*"

His point? You have to stay. You have to serve. You have to "remain under" as James said, so that endurance can have its good work in you.

As I drove back up the I-5 corridor to Portland, the thought came to me as a paraphrase of Orville's thoughts: *The only reason Jesus became a man was to be man-handled.* That's the thought that got me through the years of long days and short nights and the grinding pressure of seminary. That's the conviction that has carried me through the manifold highs and lows of ministry. I've wanted to quit many times…in fact, if I had a dollar for every time I've thought of it, I probably could afford to.

But I keep thinking about Orville, who stayed and stayed and stayed. He never left the Bride of Christ; he was called to help her become free of stain and blemish. So despite the pettiness, hard hearts, ingratitude, and slow progress of wounded human beings such as me and thee, he stayed. He endured. As Job before him, he "held fast to his integrity."

Job's enormous staying power was rooted in his walk with God. He had placed his confidence in the Living One. He did not withdraw it. The man's relationship with God was such that it generated staying power. He capsulated his confidence with a strong statement: *He knows the way with me; when he has tried me, I shall come forth as gold.* In other words, "The God I serve knows precisely what is happening in the most secret parts of my soul. He knows how much I can handle and how much I can't. I trust Him with my life. Therefore I will handle it. And when this is over, I will be even more like He wants me to be." Job must have recited that old preacher's prayer: "Lord, help me to remember that nothing is going to happen to me today that You and I can't handle together."

Staying power.

The bottom line? Stay with it, man. Stick by your commitments.

Stand by your promises. Never, never let go, no matter what.

When marriage isn't fun...*stay in it.*
When parenting is over your head...*stay at it.*
When work is crushing your spirit...*don't let it beat you.*
When the local church is overwhelmed with pettiness...*stay by it.*
When your children let you down...*pick them up.*
When your wife goes through a six-month mood swing...*live with it.*
When it's fourth and fourteen with no time on the clock...*throw another pass.*

Understand that the heart of staying power is SACRIFICE—giving one's self up for the good of another. For the ultimate example of staying power, our eyes have only to lock in on the Lord Jesus Christ. When He could have turned away from the cross, He stayed on course, setting His face like a flint, all the way to Calvary. When He could have come down from the cross and sidestepped the suffering, He stayed. When He could have summoned armies of angels to deliver Him and called down divine air strikes on His adversaries, He stayed. He persevered and "stayed under" all the way until that moment came when He could cry out, "It is finished!"

And why did He do that? So that through His resurrection power alive in our lives, you and I could become the kind of men He called us to be. We can hang in there and face anything life or death or hell has to throw at us...because He did it all before us. He not only models staying power, He provides it for the asking. He not only shows us what the Ultimate Man is like, He rolls up His sleeves and helps us get it done.

That's why real men don't run. Real men stay and stay and stay. Like Orville. Like Job. Like Jesus.

A Man Faces Himself

1. List ten major commitments you have made in your life.

How have you done with them?
Which, if any, fell by the wayside?
Why did they?
How did you stick with the commitments that grew tough?
Are *you* satisfied with your track record?

After you've spent some time thinking through these questions, stop. Get on you knees somewhere alone. Pray for at least ten minutes— ask God to strengthen you in your commitments, and to forgive you for any failures (He loves to do it!). Thank Him for His own infinite and unconditional commitment to you! Get up, walk out, face your world, and enjoy the power of promise keeping. You'll love it. Deep down.

2. Get access to an NIV Exhaustive Concordance and look up all the references to "staying power" kind of words and their derivatives such as: endure, faithful, persevere, firm. What insights do these verses give you into increasing your own "staying power"? What one thing can you do *today* to implement some of these insights?

A Man Meets with His Friends

1. Why do you think "staying power" is so little evidenced in our contemporary culture?

2. In what specific ways did Job demonstrate "staying power"? How did he acquire it? How are you following (or not following) his example?

3. If the disasters that hit Job were to happen to you, how do you think you'd respond? Explain.

4. What kind of circumstances are most likely to get you thinking about running away from family responsibilities? What keeps you from running?

5. Are you the kind of man who "swears to his own hurt, and does not change"? Can you think of an example or two of when you did?

6. Describe several men in your acquaintance who modeled "staying power."

7. What do you think of the statement, "The only reason Jesus became a man was to be man-handled"?

8. How is *sacrifice* at the heart of "staying power"?

Beneath the Breastplate:

A Man's Tender Side

Our attitude among you was one of tenderness...
(1 THESSALONIANS 2:7, PHILLIPS).

IMAGINE JOHN WAYNE diapering a baby. Or Clint Eastwood "cooing" a toddler. You pretty much *have* to imagine it. Because you've probably never seen it on the silver screen. It's not the Right Image, you know. The celluloid hard guy is hard-core. Scornful of sentiment. One dimensional. And phony as a guy in a cheap gorilla suit. Hollywood folks wouldn't know a Tender Warrior if they saw one. They get it wrong every time.

Underneath the warrior's breastplate beats a tender center. In every man there is the tender side. The side that connects to another. The thirst for relationship. The desire to touch and be touched. To hug. To link. To be *with.*

A real man has feelings and isn't afraid to express them.

Contrast Tinsel Town's John Wayne ("Never apologize, Mister, it's a sign of weakness") with real-life hero General Norman Schwarzkopf. Not long after the Gulf War and the dazzling victory over Iraq, the conquering commander of Desert Storm appeared on national television in an interview with Barbara Walters. In the course of their conversation about the war, something touched the big man. We all watched with fascination as the eyes of this career soldier with four stars on his shoulder glazed over. Tears formed.

Ms. Walters, with well-practiced bluntness, said, "Why, General, aren't you afraid to cry?"

Stormin' Norman replied without hesitation, "No, Barbara. I'm afraid of a man who *won't* cry!"

Barbara had more than she bargained for on the other end of her jaded microphone. America was witnessing the distinctive heartbeat of a Tender Warrior. I'd cheerfully follow him into the back alleys of Baghdad. Or anywhere else. Wouldn't you?

Real men long for connection, touch, and the genuine expression of feelings.

You see it every Sunday during the football season. It's there—among some of the world's biggest, strongest, most competitive men. The inner drive to touch and connect won't be denied. What's the first thing they do when a great offensive drive explodes in a touchdown?

They look for someone to touch.

Oh, sure, they call them "high-fives." But they're really hugs. I call them chicken hugs. (After all, men aren't supposed to "lose control" and *really embrace* in front of God and a national television audience, are they?) Those magnificent hulks of the gridiron long to be connected. *WE did this TOGETHER. I like you. You like me. We're teammates. We belong. Let's touch…if only for a second and just a little bit.*

It's the "tender" trying to shine through the warrior. But it's often just a momentary burst. Our false images of manliness will try to shut it down.

Now don't get me wrong. There is a difference between "tender" and *soft.* That's why they're two different words. I'm not at all advocating what Robert Bly calls the "soft male" of the 1970s. Listen to his description:

In the seventies I began to see all over the country a phenomenon that we might call the "soft male." Sometimes even today when I look out an an audience, perhaps half the young males are what I'd call soft. They're lovely, valuable people—I like them—they're not interested in harming the earth or starting wars. There's a gentle attitude toward life in their whole being and style of living.

But many of these men are not happy. You quickly notice the lack of energy in them. They are life-preserving but not exactly life-giving. Ironically, you often see these men with strong women who positively radiate energy.[1]

We want Tender Warriors…not "soft males." Webster's Dictionary nicely distinguishes between the terms. "Tender" is linked to the Latin root *tendre*, which means "to stretch out, or extend." The word itself is defined as "expressing or expressive of feelings of love, compassion, kindness; affectionate, as in 'a tender caress'; considerate; careful."

In contrast, when the word "soft" is used to describe an individual, it means "mild, effeminate, easily yielding to physical pressure; unresistant to molding, cuffing, wear; untrained for hardship."

Masculine sensitivity never will and never *should* match its feminine counterpart. The average male will never be as sensitive as the average female. Don't even try. Just accept it. Accept her highly developed, finely tuned sensitivities. The difference is part of the Creator's planned complement. So don't overdo. But do loosen up…it's a long way from macho to soft. Come down somewhere in between. Let's look at a couple of balanced examples; one contemporary, one ancient.

A Contemporary Tender Warrior

I recall one magnificent warrior from my past. He commanded one of the most powerful military units you could hope to see—a five thousand-man armored brigade. Two tank battalions. A mechanized infantry battalion, an artillery battalion, and the Third Squadron of the Twelfth Cavalry. Colonel DeWitt C. Smith knew himself well enough that he was unintimidated by "image"—his own or anyone else's. He was tall. Handsome. Articulate. A powerful leader and a soldier's soldier.

His Second Brigade of the Third Armored Division sat astride the

Fulda gap at the height of the Cold War. The traditional invasion route between eastern and western Europe, the Fulda had seen more than its share of military boots—even Napoleon's had walked its roadsides. The Soviet armored units to the east presented a formidable opponent. It was serious stuff.

A bright man (he'd been a military speech writer for President John Kennedy in an earlier assignment), Colonel Smith applied himself fully to the task. He took his mission seriously, and every man in the brigade knew it. Don't mess with the colonel. Don't mess with the mission. Don't mess up. Just don't mess, period. Get it right.

But the colonel took more than his mission seriously. He took his men seriously. He loved his soldiers. Actually loved them. I was one of them, and I felt that love. So did my wife. The tender heart of that warrior touched us in a deep and unforgettable way.

Linda was pregnant. Our first. This young fuzzy-cheeked "butter bar" (pejorative enlisted talk for "Second Lieutenant"—the scourge of the military) and his wife were going to have a baby. We were thrilled. Couldn't wait. I walked taller. Linda smiled more. Life was rich! Plans were in place. The nursery was taking shape. It was big time.

Then it happened. I was in the field with the brigade on maneuvers. Linda was alone. Ten thousand miles from home, from her mother, and from friends. She began to bleed. Then she miscarried—and my young wife's world began to spin like a crazy top—out of control. Another officer's wife with more experience in "military communication" managed to get the message to the maneuvering brigade busy at its serious work.

Colonel Smith called me to his headquarters. My commanding officer met me with a tenderness beyond anything I'd ever observed in him. (Isn't it funny how the less mature feel constrained to act "tough," while the truly mature act gently?)

In a quiet voice, with his eyes locked into mine, my "CO" began describing what had happened to Linda and our baby. He told me it hurt her. But more than the physical loss, he told me it hurt her inside—at the core of her feminine soul. Most insightfully, he spoke to me of her heart, what he anticipated she was experiencing in her soul.

He told this younger soldier, newer husband, and less experienced man what my wife would be needing in the coming hours and days.

"Lieutenant," he said, "your lady needs you right now—much more than this brigade does. In her heart, she's probably wondering if she has somehow failed. Let you down. Let herself down. Let her child down."

"Go to her," he said. "Take several days off. Stay with her. Talk to her. Reassure her. Love her."

He asked if I understood.

"Yes, sir," I said. "Thank you, sir."

I saluted and turned to go. He stopped me. With a smile and a wink, he said, "Lieutenant...tell her it isn't the end of the world. Tell her Mrs. Smith and I (who had an unusually large and healthy family—the envy of many) have suffered several miscarriages. You can do this. Your future is still very bright. Don't forget that."

With that I left—having been instructed, encouraged, and touched deeply by a Tender Warrior. I would be a better man for it. That man on a mission had allowed his tender side to provide perspective. Colonel Smith firmly believed that the whole reason we were soldiers was for our wives, our children, our nation, our way of life. Again and again through those months under his command, he showed me that without tender-hearted relationships, there was no reason for being a soldier—no reason for anything at all.

There wasn't an ounce of Hollywood in that real-life warrior. No imbalanced macho. No self-elevating bluster. No trash-talking bravado. No off-the-shelf hard-guy sneer. Move over Clint Eastwood, I'll let the colonel make my day. Any day.

An Ancient Warrior

A long time ago on the southern portion of that same European continent, another warrior fought with all his heart. His mission was less defense and more offense. He had no armored vehicles at his command, no AWACS circling the skies, no high-tech arsenal, and only a small platoon of faithful soldiers. But he paid an enormous price, fought incredible battles on a variety of fronts, and never quit—

even when faced with imminent death.

He was a warrior. A never-say-die kind of guy. He fought his way up mountains. Spent his share of time crossing valleys. Swam more than one raging river. Often crazed with thirst and without food for days, he survived sleepless nights. He fought off the cold and exposure, endured all kinds of discomfort on "troop ships" en route to the next battlefield, and overcame every imaginable kind of human stress—imprisonment, torture, betrayal, and beatings that left him an inch from death. He would have done Louis L'Amour proud. And he won more than his share of purple hearts. Listen to an entry from what might be viewed as a curl-edged page from a soldier's combat diary:

> I have worked harder than any of them. I have served more prison sentences! I have been beaten times without number. I have faced death again and again. I have been beaten the regulation thirty-nine stripes by the Jews five times. I have been beaten with rods three times. I have been stoned once. I have been shipwrecked three times. I have been twenty-four hours in the open sea. In my travels I have been in constant danger from rivers and floods, from bandits, from my own countrymen, and from pagans. I have faced danger in the city streets, danger in the desert, danger on the high seas, danger among false Christians. I have known exhaustion, pain, long vigils, hunger and thirst, doing without meals, cold and lack of clothing (2 Corinthians 11:23-27, Phillips).

The apostle Paul was a fighter. A man to ride the river with. When pushed, he wore the dangers and hardships of his mission like chevrons on his shoulder. They were his credentials. Sylvester Stallone's Rambo has nothing on him when it comes to standing up to a challenge. Our world tends to think of him as an incredibly imposing figure. A man who sent ripples not only across his own world, but into the world to come. His impact spanned centuries. He possessed an absolutely fearless spirit, strong will, and fiery persona. He was a powerful communicator. A world beater in every sense of the term.

But no one knows the heart of a man like the man himself. What do you think this battle-scarred gospel tiger saw in the mirror every morning? Want to look under his breastplate and see what was going on down deep inside the man? When the battles raged and the missiles clanged hard against his armor, how did he see himself? How would he describe his own actions? Listen.

> We proved to be gentle among you, as a nursing mother tenderly cares for her own children. Having thus a fond affection for you, we were well pleased to impart to you not only the gospel of God but also our own lives, because you had become very dear to us (1 Thessalonians 2:7-8).

Gentle? Tender care? Nursing mother? Children? Fond affection? Very dear? Does that sound like a warrior to you? Are those words you would expect from a man's man? God does. Paul says that all his hardship was ironclad "proof" of his tender love.

Let's take a little further look into that passage—at those elements underneath the breastplate. Take a good long look at the man's tender side. Paul grabs hold of a couple of the key character traits of a Tender Warrior.

Fond Affection: A Manly Sense of Connection

Paul uses a very rare expression to capture his feelings. In all the New Testament, this is the only place this term appears. "Fond affection" is a term taken from the world of the nursery and child care. It is used for the strong endearment of that most gentle of all relationships—a woman and her nursing child. Further, there seems to be a sense of dedicated professionalism attached to its usage. It describes the finest of skilled care-givers. It is that underlying sense of emotional connection required to complete any truly meaningful challenge— like raising children, for example.

The great apostle suggests that the heart of his ministry was the ministry of his heart—tender, gentle, fond, affectionate. Familial in nature, it elevates a kindred spirit. The one-for-all, all-for-one spirit of the true musketeer. It is a manly skill useful in conquering both continents and gridirons.

Let's go back to that Sunday afternoon gridiron. Sure, it's "only a game," but you'd better believe those massive men in pads and helmets take it seriously. And the best of them know that becoming a champion requires more than passing, catching, running, blocking, and tackling skills. A whole lot more. The blue-chip Sunday warriors recognize it takes *connection*, yes, even *emotional* connection—"fond affection"—to get the job done.

Coaching legend Vince Lombardi, no New Testament theologian by any stretch, but a man who knew men, certainly understood this truth. His Green Bay Packers ran over the top of everybody in professional football in the sixties. And they did it TOGETHER. Connected by "fond affection." Lombardi, their leader, insisted upon it. He said it straight forward:

> You've got to care for one another. You have to love one another. Each player has to be thinking about the next guy. The difference between mediocrity and greatness is the feeling these players have for one another. Most people call it team spirit. When the players are imbued with that special feeling you know you have yourself a winning team.[2]

A fond affection overcomes obstacles. It carries. It wins. It means literally "to feel oneself drawn to." It's the kind of emotion our Lord was experiencing when He said to His men, "I have longed to have this Passover dinner with you." Fond affection is a term of endearment. An almost uncontrollable urge to hold, to hug, to explode with the joy of togetherness.

I'll never forget the first time I saw my firstborn son. Talk about fond affection. It was in the Republic of Germany, where I was stationed in the army. Kent had just been born in the military hospital. In those days fathers were not permitted in the delivery room (an unbelievably short-sighted convention for which I still have a hard time forgiving the medical profession). They told me I could see him through the nursery glass. I flew to the window. They had lined up all the newborns in their cribs. There must have been fifteen or twenty of them. One was noticeably larger than the rest—a twenty-two-inch, nine-pound lump of humanity wrapped in a blue blanket. The card on the crib said "WEBER." This one was *mine!* There, for the first time in my life, my eyes rested on one of my own. I remember the fond affection welling up so strong I wanted to rebel against all authority—military and medical—that was keeping me from him. I had an overwhelming urge to throw a brick through that nursery window. I wanted to be with him, hold him.

Through the window my heart whispered to his, *I love you. I will do anything for you. I will never leave you. You are mine. And I am yours.*

That fond affection still drives our relationship. Just recently, almost twenty-four years after my eyes first saw him through the glass, we sat across a table from one another in a restaurant. I found myself saying out loud to this now six-foot-four, two-hundred-ten pound, fully grown man the same thing my heart had whispered through the window years before.

"I love you, Kent. I will do anything for you. I will never leave you. I am yours. And you are mine." Over the years I've sought to reinforce it with a similar statement of commitment: "Nothing you could ever do could be bad enough to turn me away from you."

My son is my friend. It's a fond affection.

Healthy Openness: A Manly Sense of Communication

With Paul it was always a matter of "what you see is what you get." Clear to the core. Open to the sight. Transparent. He was pleased to communicate far more than just "the truth." By this time in his life he was realizing some things about himself. Hard-charging and goal-oriented, he had likely hurt more than one person along the way (remember John Mark?). Now, in his masculine maturity, he demonstrates the "better way" he described to the Corinthians. Yes, he told the truth. And he did it by giving himself away. "We were pleased to *impart* to you not only the gospel (truth) of God, but also our own lives."

Interesting word, "impart."

Paul chose a compound word to describe his actions. It translates literally as *giving-again.* He gave. He gave again. More and more. Holding nothing back. In a very real sense, the apostle "gave himself away." This was a man who thought deeply, felt deeply, and gave everything he had to his friends—his thoughts and his feelings. A real man must not be afraid to tell you who he is deep down inside. Paul describes a form of communication that reaches back, back, behind the rib cage. It's a vulnerable, wide-open, unselfish, "here is my soul" communication.

The husband does it when he lets his wife into the back rooms of his soul. He tells his fears, dreams, hopes, failures, feelings, the whole "nine yards." The businessman does it when he opens his life to his co-workers. A statement attributed in my hearing to John Stemmons, an especially competent Dallas businessman, says it well. To the question "How do you build a successful business?" Stemmons reportedly replied, "You find some people who are comers, who are going to be achievers in their own field...people you can trust. Then grow old together."

That's it. Stay with each other and give yourself away—imperfections and all. That's openness. That's transparency.

If you're going to be a man after God's heart, you're not going to pretend to be perfect. Nobody is. So my kids need to know that I have needs, too. They need to understand that I'm not everything I want to be. I need to share with them not only my strengths and my "strong, silent character." I need to share with them, as they grow, my weaknesses and struggles, even failures—when it's appropriate. People around us need to know we're not Clark Kent. That life is not an exact science. We don't have it all together, and it's important that we become healthily transparent with one another.

Genuine openness is a form of spirit-to-spirit communication that defies description—let alone definition. But you know it when you see it. I recall a moment in the life of my middle son. Blake was a youngster. I was mowing our yard astride our new lawn tractor. To an eight-year-old boy, such a contraption represents nirvana. To sit on it. To steer it. To *drive* it. Well...what else is there on this earth that matters? But in this case it wasn't happening because this safety-conscious "mean ol' dad" wouldn't allow him to ride it for fear of an accident and injury.

So Blake sat on the front porch and watched me on my rounds. Elbows on knees. Head in hands. Disappointment and longing written all over his little face. His gaze followed me back and forth across the yard, like he was watching a tennis match (a very slow one). His posture cried out, *Oh, Daddy, I want to be WITH you!*

Ultimately, I could stand it no longer. This father's heart caved in. With a smile and an upraised arm, I motioned him to join me. His face burst into expression. He leaped off the porch, covering what seemed to be ten yards in a single bound. He flew to my side. Carefully, he climbed onto the seat safely between my knees. As he did, he slid forward and dropped his head back to look up at my face. I bent forward to look in his, our noses about six inches apart. His eyes literally sparkled. His soul came right to the surface. I saw deep down inside those eyes to his spirit, and he to mine. Without a word, we communicated. Deeply. *I'm with you, Dad, and you're with me. We're doing the most wonderful things together. I would rather be right here right now than any other place in the universe.*

It was a moment of open spirit communication I will never forget.

Thinking of that term "giving one's self away...again" reminds me of another incident with one of my sons; this time my youngest. Ryan is number three of three boys. By the time he came along, there weren't many worlds left to conquer. There wasn't much left for him to claim as his own. Personal identity is hard to come by when you follow in a train—especially a train of three with two pretty high-powered brothers in front of you. It's tough being a caboose.

Because we live in Oregon, the out-of-doors has become our playground. We love to hike, camp, hunt, fish, and do anything else that puts us in the mountains and forests together. In such activity, a "trusty knife" becomes a man's best friend. And usually, just when you need one, there's none to be found! Activity comes to a grinding halt until a worthy blade—or any blade at all—can be located. Hence the owner of the camp's best pocket knife becomes something of an honored guest, much sought after, much valued.

For his birthday one year I gave Ry the "best pocket knife." It was a thing of beauty. A cause for strutting. For the first time in his life, Ryan became the man of the hour. "The brothers," as he often referred to the older boys, had to come to him. For the first time in *their* lives, they had to ask him for permission for something. The Knife had immediately elevated his status in the tribe. It was heady stuff.

June 30 rolled around. It was my birthday, and I was spending the day in my study, buried in the books. I "sensed" him before I heard him. Ryan was standing behind me. I came up from my studies, spun in my chair, and turned to my boy.

He had something in his hand. A gift. Wrapped somewhat crudely but very proudly. He had chosen this time when he knew I would be alone. He didn't want anyone else around; these were moments for just the two of us. A dad, a boy, and a gift. Two spirits and an expression. Carefully, I unwrapped the treasure. You guessed it—The Knife!

My son had given and given again. He had given himself away. He had given me his heart, his identity. He wanted me to have him. We communicated, heart to heart. It was transparency. Our souls wrapped themselves around each other. No, it was not "just a knife." It was Ryan and me. Exchanging hearts. I learned a lot that day about being a man—from a boy. He had "imparted" his "very life" to me. Neither of us can ever forget it. It was a magnificently manly thing to do. In an earlier era, it would have been akin to surrendering one's own sword, hilt forward, to a fellow warrior, in token of lasting fidelity.

My youngest son's gift pierced right through my armor and passed into my chest. I carry that little knife still, lodged somewhere in the deep places of my heart. Nothing will ever remove it.

That's the way it is, when you've been bested by a Tender Warrior.

A Man Faces Himself

1. Tenderness sometimes (often!) takes planning. Design and carry out a special evening with your wife where you *intentionally* display tenderness—not eroticism, nor wimpiness.

2. Identify several godly older men in your church. Ask them what they have done in their marriages to tenderly care for their wives. Pick their brains! There's a motherload of wisdom in such men.

A Man Meets with His Friends

1. Think of the men you know best. Is it hard for them to express or discuss their feelings? Why?

2. General Norman Schwarzkopf said he was "afraid of a man who *won't* cry." What do you suppose he meant? Do you agree? Why or why not?

3. What does "masculine sensitivity" mean to you?

4. Think of the Tender Warriors in your past. What did they have in common? How were they different? How would you like to emulate them?

5. Do the terms "gentle," "tender care," "fond affection," "very dear" well describe your leadership style? Why or why not?

6. How do you "give yourself away" to the members of your family? How *often* do you do this?

7. If you were to place yourself on a "Hollywood tenderness scale" somewhere between Alan Alda (soft) and Clint Eastwood (hard), where would you land? Are you happy with your position? Explain your answer.

Under Orders:

A Man and His Leadership

You know that the rulers of the Gentiles lord it
over them...it is not so among you
(MATTHEW 20:25-26).

I T WAS ONE OF those golden seasons in life when the sun shines unfailingly warm and the wind blows unfailingly gentle. Linda and I were stationed in what was then West Germany, where I was a brigade signal officer in an armored division. We had been married less than three years, and our hearts were wrapped around each other and around our bright-eyed, red-cheeked, seven-month-old son. We didn't have much in the way of possessions, but I already had everything I'd ever wanted in life—a loving wife, a baby son, a challenging job, and an outstanding commander.

The envelope should have been no surprise.

We knew it was coming. We knew it *had* to come. Why should my heart pound and my blood run cold when I suddenly received what I knew to be inevitable? And yet...how could I ever be ready to get the ultimate orders to Vietnam? Orders sending me far away from my home and family for long, weary months. Orders that might well be sending me to dismemberment, captivity, or death.

Yet isn't this what I was trained for? Isn't this what I was made for?

Our nation was at war. What does a soldier do except go into combat?

Six weeks later we were back in Yakima, in my parents' station wagon, riding those few, silent miles to the airport. My thirty-day leave was over. Christmas was over. The golden days were over. Forever? Who could say? As the plane climbed up and away, I looked back over my right shoulder. Just for a moment, the little window framed all that was in my heart. My very life. Standing on the tarmac were my mom, my dad, my wife, and my baby. Tiny figures...soon lost from view as grey tendrils of cloud swallowed the ascending flight. I remember thinking, *Why am I doing this? I would rather be doing anything else right now. Of all the places in the world I would rather be, it's the one I'm leaving.*

Finally I had to come back to this: I was doing what I was doing for one reason; I had orders. Like the centurion in Jesus' day, I was a man under authority.

I still am.

No, I'm no longer getting envelopes from the Pentagon, but I am no less a man under authority, a man under orders. And if the Lord God has allowed you the unspeakable privilege of being a husband and father, so are you.

In his famous Horatio Hornblower novels, C. S. Forester painted unforgettable scenes of life in the eighteenth-century British navy. His famous protagonist, Captain Hornblower, would receive his orders from the Lords of the Admiralty in a sealed oilskin pouch weighted with musket balls (in the event it had to be hastily hurled into the deep to elude enemy hands). After the towering frigate or ship of the line weighed anchor and tacked majestically out of harbor, the captain would turn the bridge over to his first lieutenant and go below to his cabin in the stern.

His first official act would be to open and read the sealed orders, directing him to take command of the ship and perform certain duties and accomplish specific objectives within the weeks and months prescribed. That night, he would have his officers join him for dinner in his cabin. After the meal was cleared away, he would lay out essentials of the upcoming mission and issue appropriate orders.

Finally, clutching glasses of Hornblower's best claret, the assembled officers would rise as one man, drink to the king's health, and off they would sail to meet their destiny.

He was a man in authority. He was a man *under* authority. To shirk this captain's orders meant disgrace or death. Similarly, for the captain to forsake *his* duties as lord and commander over that compact little community of a thousand souls meant disgrace or death. He was commanded to lead; it wasn't an option.

He who is the Ultimate Authority chose to describe a man's role in the home as "head." Those were His choice of words, not mine. It is God's Word. The orders have already been delivered, once for all, to husbands and fathers. We are *commanded* to lead; it isn't optional. Speaking through the apostle, God the Holy Spirit said: "I want you to understand that Christ is the head of every man and the man is the head of a woman, and God is the head of Christ" (1 Corinthians 11:3).

Here is another passage. Same God speaking: "For the husband is the head of the wife, as Christ also is the head of the church, He Himself being the Savior of the body" (Ephesians 5:23).

What? Is that hyperbole? Or is that Scripture? What an astounding, comprehensive statement. Now before anyone "waters it down" or resorts to some linguistic gymnastics and dilutes the issue, read those verses again. And again. Pretty direct stuff.

But something is happening in our day, even among evangelical believers, that is akin to ripping down traffic signals in busy intersections across our country. And if it continues, the damage and pain will likely extend *generations* deep.

My friend Robert Lewis was waiting for a flight at the Atlanta airport when he came across a headline in the *Atlanta Journal*: "New Swiss Marriage Law Ends Men's Reign as Head of the House."[1]

The article began, "On January 1 husbands lost their position as undisputed head of the family...." Well, there you have it. I guess that pretty much sums it all up and settles the issue. So much for millennia of human history. Even Switzerland, the home of the immovable Alps and centuries of conservative tradition, has decided there must be a better way. According to the new law every issue in the home is left to individual discretion. Finances, debts, legal concerns are all purely personal matters. After all, this is the era of individual rights. The private person is king. Every man, every woman is an island. And everyone does that which is right in his own eyes ("so long as it doesn't hurt anyone else, of course"), right?

Will it work? Is it truth? Applied universally will it hold up? Let's go back to our traffic light analogy. What if the article had read like this? "On January 1 city hall lost its position as head traffic authority in our community. From this day forward the movement of individuals will be left entirely to individual discretion." Traffic signals are out. Stop signs are banished. Just do what you think best. Left turn lanes no longer exist. Decide for yourself.

What do you think? Will it work? Sounds to me like a good time to stay off the streets. We're looking at a prescription for chaos. Confusion. And incalculable damage and pain.

God has given instructions regarding those under authority:

—to everyone who is governed
—to all believers within the local church
—to wives
—to children
—to servants or employees
—AND TO HUSBANDS.

And His instructions to all are very clear:

—submit to Christ
—be subject to
—obey
—respect.

As men and husbands we must own a spirit of submission, not just a sense of technical hierarchy.

So let me ask you a question or two, men. Questions that we often ask at Family Life Marriage Conferences across the nation:

Does it bother your wife that "God is the head of Christ"?

Probably not.

Does it bother her that "Christ is the head of every man"?

No, in fact, she probably loves it and prays it will be more realized every day.

Does it bother your wife that "the man is the head of a woman"?

Most likely! Of course, it bothers her. Why is that?

It's probably half due to her sin nature...and half due to *your* sin nature. Why, in our culture, do so many discussions of male/female roles seem so painful, unfair, unreal, unfunny, and even preposterous? Because of men who demand submission from their wives but in turn submit themselves to no one, including God. We men truncate the divine process by our arrogant, foolish, egocentric, SELFishness. We cannot blame women for being frustrated because they fear the injustice of being under headship that itself is not accountable.

Some men draw a big line in the sand and say, "I ain't accountable to nobody, but I am the boss of you." That is neither right nor biblical. Yes, God has given men a certain amount of authority. But they are first and foremost men *under* authority. We always want to quote the verse that says, "The man is the head of a woman." But we conveniently forget the first part of the verse that says, "Christ is the head of every man!" No exceptions. That's me...and you.

Men, *are you coming under Christ's authority?* That's the key question of this whole chapter. If you are not accountable to Christ for your husbanding, you are as guilty as you may feel your wife to be. As a man, as a leader, as a husband, I need to go back to Scripture's admonitions *to me* that are sandwiched between the instructions to other people to submit. Am I loving my wife as myself? Am I being harsh or inconsiderate with her? Am I exasperating my children with my leadership? Am I embittering them with my unfairness? Am I submitting to the authority of my local church leaders and civil government authorities? Am I willing to submit myself to fellow Christians? I may think I'm cut out to be a good general. But have I first learned to be a good soldier? Before one can ever lead, he must learn to follow.

If I fail to live as I'm instructed, I undermine my own credibility to remind or teach my family to live as they're instructed. How can I credibly teach others to obey God if I don't? Men, you and I need to make sure we are obeying as well, and that we are providing a climate where obedience can flourish.

Such a climate begins with our own respect for and adherence to Scripture. We cannot take our cues from our culture. We must return to drink deeply from the headwaters. Christian thought springs directly from the nature of God and its revelation in His Word. Every major tenant of our faith is a matter of *revelation* not explanation. Each is a mystery to be learned no way other than by revelation. We know what we know by taking Him at His Word. We apprehend His intentions and affirm our allegiance by believing what He says. Whether it is the nature of our salvation or the nature of our homes, we take it by faith, trusting and obeying.

So let's go below decks and open that oilskin pouch containing our orders. Let's spread that parchment out on the table. There are a couple of key words we should review and ponder...the seas may get rough up ahead.

Two Words

The two words are fairly simple. Forthright. Direct. They fly in the face of our changing culture, but then, so does the Bible. Scripture has never worried itself about whose culture was in charge at the moment. The Bible deals with the intentions of the created order, not the cultural ramifications that are always in flux. These are words—benevolent words—which provide our homes with leadership, authority, order, and direction.

HUSBAND. The noun form of husband means "manager." A husband is a "steward." A caretaker. The man responsible. In its verb form the term means "to direct, to manage." Those are strong terms that imply effective leadership. In a word, husbanding is responsibility. To be a husband is to be responsible.

HEAD. "Head" means: director
                      chief
                      headmaster
                      principal
                      foremost.

"Head" equals leadership or authority, as in the head of the class, head of the military, head of the company, head of the church, head of the home. Head man. Head means head.

So, how are we doing? It's not too hard to catch the drift. In our culture, it may be hard to *swallow*, but it is not hard to understand. It all seems pretty straightforward, but does it match the biblical emphasis? Let's see if it does by walking through a few passages.

The Man Is Created First

Back at the headwaters of the Bible, the book of Genesis says in unmistakable terms that God created the man *first*. Is that a big deal? Should we draw something from that, or did it just happen—kind of a divine coincidence?

It was no coincidence. God Himself highlights it with a red marker in the New Testament when addressing the issue of authority among men and women. One of the reasons for His affirmation of male leadership is the order in which He created them. "For it was Adam who was first created, and then Eve." Male leadership is part of the original plan. It is not the result of the Fall, sin, or culture. It is the Creator's original intention. That's the way it's *supposed* to be.

Prior order says that man was created first. That fact is neither "cultural" nor sinful. Adam didn't apply for the job. No one drew straws or tossed a coin. No one interviewed for the position or took a test. Short as he was on "previous experience," Adam certainly didn't have a better resume. It has nothing to do with anything except divine design. God just wanted it that way.

Was it because the man is somehow more valuable to God? Not at all! We need to distinguish here between value and *function*. The Bible makes absolutely clear that our value as human beings, men and women, comes from the fact that we are created in the image of God. Male and female are absolutely equal in value and worth before the living God.

Equality, however, does not mean sameness. Equal does not mean identical. We have different functions just as God the Father, God the Son, and God the Spirit, while absolutely equally God, have different functions. The Father is God. The Son is God. The Spirit is God. For purposes of function or outworking we describe their relationship as one of economic trinity. That is simply a description of "the way it works." The Son subordinates Himself to the Father. He is no less God. He is no less valuable. He is no less worthy.

So the apostle, writing under inspiration of the Spirit of God, says that when it comes to the function of authority among God's people in the church, "I don't allow a woman to exercise authority over a man...for Adam was created first." Were the apostle alive today, he might be shot for saying that, or certainly vilified in the media as a small-minded bigot and a sexist. But that's the Bible. It just says it.

The Man Is Held Responsible for the Couple's Sin

The man was the leader from Day One. He was the head. He was the responsible one, *and God holds him responsible.* No wriggling out from under it. In the garden of Eden the man is personally brought to account for the couple's sin. The New Testament affirms Adam's culpability as a critical point of doctrine. "Just as through one man sin entered into the world, and death through sin...the judgment arose from one transgression...." (Romans 5:12,16). Eve ate of the fruit first. Adam followed. But it is for *Adam's* sin the race is condemned.

Our western, democratic, "I'm-my-own-man" way of thinking doesn't like it that way. But that's the way it is in the Bible. Corporate solidarity. The man, as head, was responsible for all his little family did or failed to do. We may think it's not "fair." After all, she took of the fruit first. What *we* think is "fair," however, is irrelevant. *What the Bible says* is what's relevant. Adam is evidently held responsible for his failure to be the man he was intended to be. Apparently, he did not provide, protect, teach, and care well. Could it be that Adam, at that point, elected to be a passive male who stepped to the background, allowed his wife to be deceived, and was held responsible for it?

Elisabeth Elliot traces distinct relational patterns in the garden account which illuminate where woman stands in relation to man:

1. She was made *for* the man. According to specifications, she was divinely designed to fit his needs exactly—an adapter, a responder.

2. She was made *from* the man, quite literally, constructed out

of one of his own bones. He was her reason for being, her *source*, which is one of the root meanings of the New Testament word for "head." If you miss the point in Genesis 2, you can pick it up in 1 Corinthians 11: "For man was not made from woman, but woman from man. Neither was man created for woman, but woman for man" (1 Corinthians 11:8-9, RSV).

3. She was brought *to* the man. God made a present of Eve to Adam, not of Adam to Eve. She was his.

4. She was named *by* the man. The Old Testament authority to name was of immense importance. It signified the acceptance of responsibility. He was taking charge.[2]

And that's the Bible. Pretty forthright. Pretty simple. But we still "kick against the goads."

Not only is the man held responsible for the couple's sin and the race condemned because of its head, but God seems to indicate in those earliest chapters that the tensions will continue. In Genesis 3 He shows the way roles will continue.

Speaking to the woman, He says, "And your desire shall be for your husband yet he shall rule over you" (3:16, literal rendering). It is a statement weighted with significance. The little word translated here as "yet" is an adversative signifying an opposition or contrast between the first and last parts of the statement. On the one hand is "her desire." On the other is his "rule over."

What might her "desire" be? What is that "desire" which stands in contrast or opposition to his designated "rule"? Several possibilities have been suggested in a wide assortment of Christian literature. But none seems to fit the context so well as the one that is greatly reinforced by an identical linguistic construction in chapter 4.

Notice Genesis 4:7. Speaking of the power of sin in human lives the text describes sin as "crouching at the door" ready to pounce upon the unwary human. The next sentence is identical in Hebrew language construction to our phrase in 3:16—"its desire is for you, but [yet] you must master it." In chapter 3 a woman's desire is contrasted with a man's designated rule. In chapter 4 sin's desire is contrasted with the necessity of man's mastering or ruling it. The passage seems to suggest that it is a woman's tendency or desire to take the leadership role, but a man must lead or "rule." It is God's created design and stated intention that the man lead.

At this point in my understanding, I believe God is saying that there is a natural desire (it's only human) on the woman's part to rule, yet if the order is to be observed and the creative design fulfilled, the man must continue to serve as head. He must actively *lead.* He must not stand passively by (as apparently Adam did earlier). If he does so, he invites the kind of disaster which has already overtaken the original family in the garden and which has potentially stalked every family since. We are all too familiar with the generational fallout of a family impacted by a passive husband and a dominant wife. The phenomenon observed in this single verse of Scripture may explain a lot of tension throughout human history, and capsulizes much of the current gender wars scarring our own culture.

Men, as husbands you have been given a trust—a stewardship, a responsibility, a duty—to husband, or manage, or care for the gifts of your wife. *If you abuse that trust, you fail at the very heart of your manhood.* In effect, if you abuse the trust, you die. Adam did, and Adam died. It's part of the deathly nature of sin and disobedience. Let me put it a little more bluntly—if you lay a hand on a woman, you should be shot, okay? A woman was made to be provided for, protected, and cared for. A man was made to be a provider, protector, and care-giver. Nothing is more pitiful than a man forfeiting his masculinity or a woman her femininity by transgressing the created order.

Our culture is so horribly confused at this point. Many are being swept away by the whirlpool of role confusion. I personally believe the more militant side of the feminist movement is a frustrated revolt against unmanly men—men with little or no concept of providing, protecting, mentoring, and loving—against tyrant men who have abused their caring responsibilities.

Recently I received a letter from a vivacious, intelligent woman in our church. I had preached a sermon on the value of leadership—servant-hearted, biblical, Tender Warrior kind of leadership. She wrote: "I know now why my husband is such a good leader...because he first learned to be a good follower." She described his career in the Marines. Admitting that their marriage had experienced its "ups and downs," she suggested that most of the ups were because of his gentle, determined leadership and most of the downs were because "I wanted to be the leader sometimes." She added, "What a wonderful day it was for me when I finally let him lead."

She went on to describe several intense, pressure-laden crises that had enveloped their family over the past year or two. She concluded: "Through it all, his leadership, honesty, fairness, integrity, and respect for God's Word have been the glue that has held it together.... He is sometimes embarrassed at his lack of Scripture knowledge and eloquent speech, but his heart knowledge and love for people can stand alone. I've always called him 'my diamond in the rough.' He may be rugged on the outside but he's tender and gentle on the inside."

She closed her letter to me with these words: "Thank you for taking the time to read this and letting me tell you what a blessing it is to be married to my own personal hero!"

Yes! She has a man. A real man. And she knows it. A Tender Warrior.

A few days after receiving her letter, I ran into the two of them at a basketball game. She had given her husband a copy of the letter. We agreed together that of all the medals he had won in the Marine Corps, wonderful as they were, none could hold a candle to the award this grateful woman had given to her husband. The medal of *honor* and *respect.*

In contrast to that story, I recently heard about a candid interview with Oregon's feisty, feminist governor, Barbara Roberts. The governor allowed the interviewer a rare glimpse into a period in her life when the world looked very different to her. She was a young wife and mother with two small children. At some point early in the marriage, that little home was changed forever when her first husband walked away. Suddenly alone and unprotected, Mrs. Roberts had to roll up her sleeves and like countless other courageous single mothers in our culture, make her own way in the world. As she encountered what she regarded as prejudice and unfairness in "the system," she burned with anger. She learned to become a fighter. She fought for her children. She fought for herself. She's been fighting ever since. How different the story might have been for this woman, her family, and many other people if one man had lived up to his God-ordained role.

The pattern of masculine leadership and feminine responsiveness is well established in Scripture. It is also very conspicuous in our world. Stephen Clark, a historian from Yale University, observes:

> Men bear primary responsibility for the larger community. Women bear primary responsibility for domestic management and rearing of young children. Every known society, past or present, assigns to the men a primary responsibility for the government of the larger groupings within the society, and assigns to the women a primary responsibility for the daily maintenance of household units and the care of the younger children.[3]

In our suspicious culture people might expect such a statement from a male sociologist. But Sherry Ortner, feminist scholar, states it even more emphatically:

> The universality of female subordination, the fact that it exists within every type of social and economic arrangement and in societies of every degree of complexity, indicates to me that we are up against something very profound, very stubborn, something we cannot root out simply by rearranging a few tasks and roles in the social system, or even by reordering the whole economic structure.[4]

> I would flatly assert that we find women subordinate to men in every known society. The search for a genuinely egalitarian, let alone matriarchal, culture has proved fruitless.[5]

We're dealing with something very fundamental here. Masculine headship is universally present. It is the anthropological standard. It is the historical practice. Most importantly, it is the scriptural mandate. How then should we respond to it? Accept it and live it. Trust it and obey it. Take the orders, and follow them. As men under authority.

"It is painful, being a man, to have to assert the privilege, or the burden, which Christianity lays upon my own sex. I am crushingly aware of how inadequate most of us are, on our actual and historical individualities, to fill the place prepared for us."

C.S. LEWIS
from *God in the Dock*

Still, many in our culture kick against it. It is campaigned against. It is mocked. It is ridiculed. It is legislated out of fashion. But it will persist. Manhood is here to stay. How tragic though that some Christians, who reputedly accept the authority of Scripture, would resist it.

So What's the Solution to the Confusion?

The solution is manly love. Men must develop a thorough, biblical, manly love. Now what is that? In a word—*headship*. It is leadership with an emphasis upon responsibility, duty, and sacrifice. Not rank or domination. No "I'm the boss" assertion. Most people who have to insist that they are the leader, usually aren't. "Husbands, love your wives *[exactly]* as Christ also loved the church *and gave Himself up for her.*" Harsh dominance is not the way of Christ.

Note the linkage. Headship is linked to saviorship. The heart of saviorship is sacrifice. The key to leadership is serving—not "lording it over."

So color your headship in soft shades of the tender side—

  providing
    protecting
      teaching
        caring
          guiding
            loving
              developing
                freeing
                  sacrificing
                  leading

rather than in the harsh tones of the warrior side—

  ruling
    presiding
      directing
        determining
          bossing
            deciding.

The essence of the tender tones is servanthood. The mature husband understands servant-leadership. Just like Jesus.

What does a healthy man look like? I can't help but recall a statement from a young guy who lives near us—a sixteen-year-old high school sophomore. His parents divorced when he was eight years old. His father left and has never returned. His stepdad, a tyrannical and poor excuse for a man, treats him poorly. Tells him to "shut up" all the time. Tells him he's worthless, stupid, and will never amount to anything.

But just ask the boy about his dream and his eyes will light up. This is what he'll tell you...

I'd like to find out where my real dad lives. And I'd like to move in next door without him knowing who I was. And...I'd like to just become his friend. Once I had become his friend, then maybe it would be okay for me to move on.

This same young man who has had all kinds of difficulty in his life was asked to write an essay on the subject: "What is a man?" The following is his brief essay...written by a boy who has never really been around a man, never really seen one. But I think there is something so inherent, so ingrained, so intrinsic, so fundamental, that even a young boy who has never seen it modeled can put it into words. Here's what he wrote:

A real man is kind.
A real man is caring.
A real man walks away from silly macho fights.
A real man helps his wife.
A real man helps his kids when they are sick.
A real man doesn't run from his problems.
A real man sticks to his word and keeps his promises.
A real man is honest.
A real man is not in trouble with the law.

It's one lonely boy's vision of a man who *stays*. A man who is both in authority and under authority.

It's a vision of a Tender Warrior.

A Man Faces Himself

1. Drop by the library (go ahead, it won't hurt). Check out a biography of a revered leader such as Abraham Lincoln or Winston Churchill. Note his use of and response to authority. What traits did he exhibit which you could emulate? Identify them. Develop a mental plan for incorporating these traits into your own life.

2. Take one of your kids aside for an hour in the evening or on a Saturday. Ask your child to assume the role of "daddy." You be the child. Ask them what they might like you to change or improve when you're the dad again. See how it feels to come under such authority.

A Man Meets with His Friends

1. What do you think it means to be "a man under authority"? In what areas of your life are you such a man?

2. What does it mean to be the "head" of a household? How do you express your leadership in the home?

3. What does it mean to be under the authority of Christ? Do you think He is pleased with your day-to-day response to His authority? Why or why not?

4. Do you think it was fair that God held Adam responsible for the first couple's sin? Explain your answer. What implications does God's action carry for your own home?

5. When power struggles erupt between you and your wife, how are they generally resolved? Are you happy with this state of affairs? Why or why not?

6. How do you express "manly love" to your wife? How could you express it better?

7. Re-read and discuss the sixteen-year-old's essay on a "real man" found on page 97. Do you agree with his conclusions? Explain.

CHAPTER SEVEN

The Rest of the Story:

A Man and His Lady, Part 1

This is now bone of my bones, and flesh of my flesh;
She shall be called Woman, because she was taken out of Man
(GENESIS 2:23).

I REMEMBER A FEW things about kindergarten. The little mats, the cookies and milk, the coat racks…and the girls. I don't recall any individuals. Just "the girls." It was my first experience with a "bunch of girls." Mrs. Taylor, our teacher, worked hard at helping us adjust to our new surroundings—seated us boy-girl-boy-girl, staggered the lines, and worked at joint games. But at recess the guys still hung out together. As did the girls. It was the same way in junior high—boys on one side of the dance floor, girls on the other.

Sometimes I chuckle at social occasions—like wedding receptions, for example—when I see adult men standing, glass in hand, on one side of the room and the women, similarly, gathered in little knots on the other. It's the junior high dance all over again.

We're just different that way, aren't we? More comfortable initially with our own kind. Not at odds, just different.

Another observer noted it long ago:

What are little boys made of?
> Frogs and snails and puppy dog tails,
> That's what little boys are made of.

What are little girls made of?
> Sugar and spice and other things nice,
> That's what little girls are made of.

Boys and girls, men and women, are...different. It doesn't take a brain surgeon or a clinical psychologist or a family therapist to tell us that. We were just kids in Mrs. Taylor's kindergarten class. But we knew there was a difference. And somehow we knew our differences ran a lot deeper than a few modifications in the plumbing systems.

The Bible notes the difference "in the beginning" of Genesis. The expression of that difference may very well be the first thing to reach our ears when we emerge from the womb—"It's a boy!" "It's a girl!" From earliest hazy memories, our "boyness" or "girlness" shapes and defines how we view life and understand ourselves.

Maybe that's why I will never forget the January 20, 1992, cover of *Time* magazine. It may be the strangest cover I have ever seen. The picture on the front isn't strange: Two youngsters smile out at you—a boy and a girl. The little boy proudly flexes his biceps while the little girl eyes him admiringly. The bold headline below the picture asks: "Why Are Men and Women Different?" The subhead below proudly announces: "New Studies Show They're Born That Way."

No kidding?

Well, blow me over! That's "news"? That's "new"? Ah, the wonders of modern research. We have finally proven in the halls of science what we already knew in the hallways of kindergarten. Having invested a great deal of money, many years of research, and a lot of energy—having scaled those formidable mountains of scientific data—we have at last pulled ourselves up over the last remaining ridge to arrive at the summit...only to discover what every mother has always known.

Boys and girls, men and women, are
  simply
      naturally
          profoundly
              unquestionably
                  thoroughly
                      DIFFERENT.

Not one better than the other. Nor worse. Just different. From day one.

This difference is so momentous that we're going to spend the bulk of two chapters on it. It accounts for a lot. Why men "just don't get it." Why women "just don't get it," either. Why our culture is in the midst of a gender war. And why your home sometimes feels like a war zone, too.

When a man and a woman begin to accept their "differentness," they can begin to accept and appreciate one another. The key to appreciating one another as man and woman is understanding and accepting your masculine-feminine differences.

What a Difference a Day Makes

Linda and I were traveling in Israel some years ago. One day in the midst of our tour was particularly stressful. We had to link up with our transportation at several locations and at numerous times throughout the day, and all on an uncomfortably tight schedule. Our itinerary called for visiting several key sites in widely scattered areas. It was a big day. The kind of day a man loves to *conquer*. Charge through. Accomplish.

That was the good news.

Unfortunately, we found ourselves in the vicinity of Jerusalem's colorful open marketplace. That meant a number of key shops to "visit." Just the kind of day a woman loves to savor. Linger over. Enjoy.

That was the bad news.

Conquering and savoring are not really compatible—at least not at the same time. Charging through and lingering, are—to say the least—quite different approaches to the same thing. It was not an easy day...you can fill in the blanks. It was tight. I was tight. She was tight.

But, hey, we got through it! We did it. Checked it off the list. Conquered. It was over. Or so I thought.

Evening shadows have a way of following the heat of the day. And just as big rocks on a sun-splashed hillside soak up the daylight warmth and radiate its heat under the stars, so the events of a day tend to color what transpires after sundown. Especially if you happen to be a woman.

That night we were staying in Galilee. Linda and I walked along that ancient shore as stars began to speckle the gathering darkness. We sat together on a large flat rock and took in the magnificence of the moment. The Milky Way swept across the clear night sky. The water lapped gently at our feet. The setting felt pretty romantic. So did the man.

I put my hand on her shoulder, gently pulling her toward me. She seemed...well, a little unyielding.

I whispered in her ear, "Honey, I really love you."

And she said, "Oh, really?"

Uh-oh. This wasn't shaping up to be the evening I had in mind.

She added, "It takes work to love me, you know."

There went the moment. Like air out of a balloon, the magic was gone. What had happened earlier that day was ancient history to me. Not to Linda. Men and women are different. And Linda was right—loving someone "different" is hard work.

That little episode in Israel, multiplied a million times a day from Galilee to Glasgow, from Katmandu to Kalamazoo, illustrates one of the most basic differences between a man and a woman. Men are compartmentalized. Focused. One thing at a time. What happened in the kitchen has no connection to the bedroom.

But women are *connected*. Comprehensive. Especially when it comes to relationships. Everything comes and goes together. What happened in the morning has everything to do with what happens in the evening. Men tend to be task oriented. Women tend to focus on relationships.

Visible from my second-floor office window are two outdoor basketball courts, occupied at recess by the kids in our church's K-8 school. One day two games were taking place simultaneously. The contrast between the girls' and boys' games illustrates the point here. The boys' game was vigorous, competitive—and rough. Bodies would fly, crash to the asphalt, and lie there—some writhing in apparent pain—but the contest went on without a moment's interruption. The injured player was forgotten. The game must go on.

The girls, seemingly with less self-esteem vested in winning, appeared to be actually enjoying *each other* during the game. At one point, there was something of a "crash" with one young lady slipping momentarily to the pavement. Immediately the girls' game halted. All nine remaining players ran to the side of their downed comrade. The little outdoor court was suddenly filled with concern, compassion, and condolences. The game itself was forgotten. The relationship must be cared for.

And it doesn't seem to change with age. My wife has a good friend who is a fine racquetball player. She and her sister, both in their forties, play a pretty good game of skill. Playing each other one day, they so enjoyed one another that the court was filled with statements of congratulation and affirmation.

"Oh, great shot, *great* shot!"

"Excellent judgment."

"You're really on target today."

They play hard, both are competitive, but,... "We talk a lot when we play. And we really laugh a lot."

In one of their recent contests they noticed a man on the balcony watching their game. Finally, during a break in the play, he just couldn't restrain himself from making a comment. "You know, ladies, you play a pretty good game. If you'd knock off the chitchat and get down to business you could have quite a contest. You'd be really good racquetball players if you didn't talk and laugh so much during your game. I've never seen anyone play quite like this."

He had missed the point of their game! It really had only a little to do with racquetball, scoring, and skills. But it had everything to do with each other and their relationship as sisters and friends.

Now the fact that men are focused on the task, achievement, and getting the job done should be no surprise. It's part of being a provider and protector. And the fact that women concentrate on relationships should be no surprise, either. It's part of being a helpmate. Those clear, unmistakable male and female differences are woven through the whole fabric of Scripture. The Bible makes it clear from the "get go" that a woman is made to relate, to connect, to respond. She is a "helpmate." But let's not get ahead of the story. Come with me back to the Garden.

Something Missing in Eden

The Living One has been having a ball creating. Earth. Sun. Moon. Stars. Creatures—myriads of them, in a million shapes, sizes, and colors. In His own words, it has been nothing but "good." But He is bothered. There is one "not good."

"It is not good for the man to be alone" (Genesis 2:18).

Now Adam hadn't figured that out yet. From his rather limited experience, Adam thought life was rolling along just grandly. Hey, this was paradise. The world smelled new. There was plenty to eat. That was all before God started the parade down Main Street. It was a parade of animals, and that was fun, too, for a while. There they came, waiting to be named, admired, and applauded. There they came, two by two...by two...by two...by two...by two. It wasn't long before this newly minted human being got the picture. He was alone! Flat out by himself. He had no counterpart. All other creatures came in pairs. He did not.

The first little tendrils of loneliness stole across his heart. Life had been full, full, full. What was this place in his chest that felt empty?

Ever been alone? I mean really alone. For a long time? There is nothing worse than aloneness. It is sheer terror. That's why solitary confinement borders on the cruel and unusual. And why it is so effective in breaking down a P.O.W. The Lord had said it all, "It is not good for the man to be alone." And now Adam knew it, too.

So the Lord finished the sentence with a great promise, "I will make a helpmate suitable for him." And He did. The Creator didn't just snap his fingers and come up with something. In the words of Scripture, He "fashioned" her. He sculpted her. He paid attention to the lines. He worked at it. He created a work of art—mentally, emotionally, physically, and spiritually. She was a "helpmate suitable."

Ladies, take no offense here. "Helpmate" is no inferior title. It describes no lesser being. As we often say at the Family Life Marriage Conferences where Linda and I serve on the speaker team, it is not "helper" in the way we might say "plumber's helper." The term says more about the one needing help (the man) than it does about the one helping (the woman). It implies the man is incomplete. *He needs help.* The God of the universe loves to describe Himself in similar terms—He is our "help" in times of trouble.

"Helper" is a majestic term. And woman is a helper "suitable" or corresponding to the man. That's another way of saying she is no duplicate. Not the same. Not a clone. A woman is not a man with redesigned plumbing. There is no redundancy here. She is Woman. Glorious. Beautiful. Creative. And different. Adam did not need a buddy, a fishing partner, or another guy to race elephants with. Man needed woman. She is "the rest of the story."

But Our Culture Doesn't Accept Differences

Our culture is constantly trying to tell us there *is* no fundamental difference between men and women. "Equality" is the name of the game. And intelligent people everywhere have to agree—men and women are absolutely equal in value.

But, as we noted earlier, equality is not sameness! To make it so is the lie of the Evil One. How ironic that a culture that espouses "the wonders of diversity" shies away from its most obvious and beautiful form. In our unbridled enthusiasm for "equality" we go to any lengths to minimize the magnificent differences between men and women. But it just won't work. Equality is not achieved by using the same scales or insisting on the same standards. The key word for a man and a woman learning to live well together is "different."

Just how different are we?

One gifted woman, Dr. Joyce Brothers, says it clearly:

Are men and women really so different? They are. They really are. I've spent months talking to biologists, neurologists, geneticists, research psychiatrists, and psychologists. What I discovered was that men are more different from women than I had known. Their bodies are different. Their minds are different. Men are different from the very composition of their blood to the way their brains develop, which means they think and experience life differently from women.[1]

More importantly, God says it quite clearly—"male and female He created them." Two different words. Two different genders. Two different creatures. No gray, drab world for God. He said, in effect, "Let's dress it up." And women have been doing the same ever since—making things beautiful. Hanging curtains on the bare windows of earth.

Dr. Brothers, writing almost as though she senses some prophetic unction or supernatural revelation, tries to help us see the light:

It's almost become an article of faith in recent years to maintain that there are no significant differences between the sexes apart from the most obvious and cherished differences. The fact is that there are other and more important differences between the sexes than the male and female reproductive organs.[2]

Dr. Paul Popenoe draws specific distinctions for us:

Men and women differ in every cell of their bodies. This difference in the chromosome combination is the basic cause of development into maleness and femaleness as the case may be.

Women have greater constitutional vitality, perhaps because of this chromosome difference. Normally, they outlive men by three or four years, in the U.S....

Women's blood contains more water (20% fewer red cells). Since these supply oxygen to the body cells, she tires more easily and is more prone to faint. Her constitutional viability is therefore strictly a long-range matter. When the working days in British factories, under wartime conditions, were increased from 10 to 12 hours, accidents of women increased 150%, of men not at all.[3]

Dr. Richard Restak, neurologist at Georgetown University School of Medicine, further clarifies some of the differences between men and women:

> Girls speak sooner, have larger vocabularies, rarely demonstrate speech defects, exceed boys in language abilities, and learn foreign languages more easily.... Boys have better total body coordination but are poorer at detailed hand activity, e.g., stringing beads.... Of eleven subtests for psychological measurements in...the most widely used general intelligence test, only two (digit span and picture arrangement) reveal similar mean scans for males and females. There are six differences so consistent that the standard battery of this intelligence test now contains a masculinity-femininity index to offset sex-related proficiencies and deficiencies.[4]

Scripture, social research, and scientific data all support the fact that very significant differences exist between men and women. But our culture does not want to accept it.

Gloria Steinem, a pioneer in the modern feminist movement, reflects the attitude of many feminists:

> We are human beings first with minor differences from men that apply largely to the act of reproduction. The only functional difference between men and women is the woman's ability to give birth; therefore a woman needs a man like a fish needs a bicycle.

In Gloria's world it seems women don't need men and men don't need women. Hers must be a lonely world. A needy world. And ultimately such a world is a self-destructive, even suicidal world. Listen to Anastasia Toufexis:

> When men try to kill themselves, it is commonly out of an injured sense of pride or competence, often related to work. When women attempt suicide, it is usually because of failures involving lovers, family, or friends.[5]

That statement offers a powerful insight into femininity as "the rest of the story." It is the same primary quality that the Creator was registering when He said, "It is not good for man to be alone." That's our first biblical clue as to the nature of woman. She originates out of man...and his need. As the Scripture puts it, "Woman was made for man, not man for woman." In Adam's need we see the first or basic quality of womanhood or femininity. A woman hates aloneness and fights it. Listen to Toufexis again:

> The reality is that women experience life differently from men; consequently, they think differently. In the words of Harvard psychologist, Carol Gilligan...they have "a different voice."
>
> At the crux of women's existence, the researchers contend, is the sense of relationship, the interconnectedness of people....
>
> Relationship colors every aspect of a woman's life.... Women use conversation to expand and understand relationships; men use talk to convey solutions, thereby ending conversations. Women tend to see people as mutually dependent; men view them as self-reliant. Women emphasize caring; men value freedom. Women consider actions within a context, linking one to the next; men tend to regard events as isolated....[6]

That explains a lot, doesn't it? What may seem like chitchat to a man is *lifeblood* to a woman. A woman sees everything as connected and therefore describes it that way. Or, as a man might say, she takes forever to "get to the point." On the other hand, a man is always striving to "get to the bottom line" and cut away what he considers "nonessential" information.

On more than one occasion Linda and I have been involved in one of those "long and pointless" (from a man's perspective) conversations that didn't seem to be going anywhere. My patience generally lasts only so long before I get fidgety. Linda frequently picks up on it before I do.

I can remember one occasion when that aspect of our conversing seemed particularly difficult for me. As Linda went into great detail about something, I found myself inwardly willing her to *get to the point.* Everything inside me was just tingling "on pins and needles" to get moving, to wrap it up, to come to a conclusion, to quit circling the field and *land* that airplane.

Linda smiled knowingly. "You would like to be excused from this conversation, wouldn't you?"

She had read my mind. We both chuckled.

Similarly, when we are driving somewhere with another couple, one of the women will often open a conversation. Soon she is telling a story about some event in the recent past. Frequently I find myself struggling to figure out how in the world this story got into this conversation about this particular topic. There doesn't seem to be a lot of connection, if any at all. I can't tell where the conversation is going, let alone how it may relate to what we're doing now. I keep waiting for the other shoe to fall. I keep waiting for the "so what?" To me, all of those unconnected details are irrelevant. To my wife, they are utterly relevant.

How so? Because, she would explain, we are sharing what is on our minds. That makes it relevant. We are together. No, there is no "big point," per se. There doesn't need to *be* a big point. No decision is required. No conclusion is called for. No logical tie-ups are needed or desired. We are just together and we're sharing our hearts. And that is enough.

Yes, men and women are different. And that very difference combats aloneness.

The Aloneness Fighter

A woman is a companion. She is a friend. *She is an aloneness fighter.* A woman will do anything to fight isolation, to combat separation, to overcome aloneness. You've seen that almost every day in your own life, haven't you?

I've had the privilege of living with Linda for over twenty-five years. When I think of all the qualities I appreciate about my wife, I value most her determination not to allow us to drift apart. But at times it's uncomfortable for me. As a man, there are times when I simply want "my space." And sometimes it has felt as if she is right there in my face. On occasion it has annoyed me that she is always "right there." But she *is* right there. She was made to be right there! She is *woman.* She is magnificently woman. Left to myself I think I would be just that—left to myself, like some bearded, wild-eyed hermit in a back-country lean-to. But the Creator wisely said, "It is not good for the man to be alone."

My wife won't allow me to be isolated. She has become a companion and friend—most often through sheer dogged determination. Fighting aloneness.

Oftentimes to a man, a woman's commitment to battling isolation, her dedication and zeal in combating aloneness, comes across as "nagging." It isn't, but it feels that way. It is actually just a difference in male and female perspective. Learning to see and appreciate those differences will go a long way toward disarming the gender wars in our culture and the skirmishes in your home.

Early in our marriage I really struggled with this. We were married the summer after my junior year and her freshman year in college. That senior year was a busy one for me, finishing up the college experience. There was a lot to conquer and not a lot of time for lingering— at least from my immature perspective. In addition to the normal classroom load, I was the football captain, the Cadet Brigade Commander in the ROTC program, traveled in a singing group that represented the college, and was finishing up my private pilot's license. I didn't know what "macho" was then, but I had the full-blown disease.

Often while walking across the campus together, Linda would want to hold hands. But my personal and masculine insecurities made it uncomfortable for me. Failing to appreciate her thirst for companionship, I would tend to pull my hand away. Thinking I had to project some kind of football-military-flyboy-tough-guy image, I held her at a distance. Put her off. I mean, *what would "the guys" think?* How would John Wayne feel about this? I never saw him hold hands in public.

Boy, was I ignorant. Completely foolish. Without realizing it I was wounding the very heart I thought I was willing to die for. Faithful in all the "big things," I was killing her in the little touches. I loved her for a lifetime, I just didn't do so well each day. You know what I mean.

Ah, but life is so daily. And so is my wife. My gracious Lord knows I need that. I'm "out there" climbing trees like

As unto the bow the cord is
    So unto man is woman;
Tho' she bends him,
    She obeys him.
Tho' she draws him,
    Yet she follows;
Useless each without the other.

HENRY W. LONGFELLOW
from "Hiawatha"

Flint McCullugh, looking ahead, squinting into the horizon, and planning way down the line. Then Linda reminds me, "I really do look forward to the future with you, but I don't care so much what lifestyle we will have in twenty years. *I want to live with you today.*"

We men can conquer mountains and do large things, but we tend not to do as well at the daily living together and fighting aloneness. Thank God for women! Thank God for the feminine perspective on living relationally. Today I am so very grateful that Linda does not like to walk alone. As recently as last night she said to me, "I like your attention."

Dinah Craik said it so well over a century ago:

Oh, the comfort,
the inexpressible comfort
of feeling safe with another person.
Having neither to weigh thoughts
nor measure words,
but pouring them all right out
just as they are,
chaff and grain together—
Certain that a faithful hand
will take and sift them,
keep what is worth keeping
and with a breath of kindness
blow the rest away.

The Nurturer of Life

A woman is more than an aloneness fighter. A strong indication of her heart appears in Genesis 3:20. Adam gives her a name that is at once very personal and revealing. "Now the man called his wife's name Eve, because she was the mother of all the living."

Her very name highlighted her life-giving role. Before they ever painted the nursery or started their family, Adam saw that his new bride's femininity was focused on mothering. He saw in her a nurturing quality that this world desperately needs.

Equipped with strong relational skills and acute interpersonal sensitivities, a *woman is a developer of life.* She builds human beings. Yes, her body is equipped to reproduce biologically. But, once again, the visible, physical properties are merely a reflection of the invisible spiritual realities. Her nature is to nurture. She communicates very naturally at the soulish level. Blessed are the children who grow up with a woman who knows who she is—proving her femininity with her family before spending it away from the home.

During the height of the feminist revolution in the seventies, talk of such inborn differences in the behavior of men and women was clearly unacceptable. As a culture we experienced what in other addictive circles would have been called "classic denial." We went to any length to deny any apparent difference between the sexes. Christine Gorman writes:

> Men dominated fields like architecture and engineering, it was argued, because of social, not hormonal, pressures. Women did the vast majority of society's child rearing because few other options were available to them. Once sexism was abolished, so the argument ran, the world would become a perfectly equitable, androgynous place, aside from a few anatomical details.

> But biology has a funny way of confounding expectations. Rather than disappear, the evidence for innate sexual differences only began to mount.... Researchers found subtle neurological differences between the sexes both in the brain's structure and in its functioning. In addition, another generation of parents discovered that despite their best efforts to give baseballs to their daughters and sewing kits to their sons, girls still flocked to dollhouses while boys clambered into tree forts. Perhaps nature is more important than nurture after all.[7]

Scripture has always indicated a woman is more suited to nurturing children than a man. How doubly unfortunate that, while secular sources continue to experience something of a conversion in the area of understanding male-female differences, "evangelical feminists" seem to continue to live in denial.

Of Buffaloes and Butterflies

What have we said so far? Before we leave this chapter, let's step back a pace or two from the details—outside the research and studies—and look at the big picture. Let's climb to the top of a tall tree and scan the horizon. It can be a healthy exercise. In general...what are the tendencies of men and women? Of course, there are exceptions, but the rule is not determined by the exception.

Men tend to be tough and strong. Women tend to be tender and gentle.

A man tends toward logic and linear thinking. A woman tends toward emotion and verbal communication.

A man tends to be a risk taker, ready to "go for it." A woman generally prefers security and order.

A man tends toward relational insensitivity, a woman toward sensitivity.

A man looks toward the long haul. A woman is concerned about here and now.

A man tends to be more skeptical and suspicious (I think it's the protector in him). A woman tends to be more believing and trusting (I think it's the nurturer in her).

Author and speaker Gary Smalley really nails down some of these general characteristics in his somewhat whimsical "buffalo and butterfly" comparison:

> The butterfly has a keen sensitivity. It is sensitive to the slightest breeze.... It notices the beauty of even the tiniest of flowers. Because of its sensitivity, it is constantly aware of all the changes going on around it and is able to react to the slightest variation in its environment. Thus, the butterfly reacts with swiftness toward anything that might hurt it. (Try to catch one without a net sometime.) If a tiny pebble were taped to its wing, the butterfly would be severely injured and eventually die.[8]

That is a powerful portrayal of the feminine side. Equally graphic is the description of the buffalo:

> The buffalo is another story. It is rough and calloused. It doesn't react to a breeze. It's not even affected by a thirty-mile-an-hour wind. It just goes right on doing whatever it was doing. It's not aware of the smallest of flowers, nor does it

appear to be sensitive to slight changes in its environment. Tape a pebble to the buffalo's back and he probably won't even feel it.

The buffalo isn't "rotten to the core" just because he goes around stepping on pretty flowers. In fact, the buffalo's toughness is a tremendous asset. His strength, when harnessed, can pull a plow that four grown men can't pull… [the man] may tend to plow through circumstances, while [the woman] may "feel" life and [her] surroundings with much more sensitivity.[9]

In our wise Creator's providence, these differences were intended to be pleasurable, effective, and even fun. As I was sitting at my desk and preparing this chapter, in fact, my lady came waltzing into the study, looked over my shoulder, and put her arms around my neck. With a knowing little smile on her face, she teased, "Did the buffalo enjoy buying the butterfly that new coat yesterday?"

She was just seeking to stretch this old buffalo's capacity to enjoy the daintier side of life.

Yes, let's enjoy the differences. Let's capitalize on them. Let's fight the temptation to say, "This is more valuable than that." Let's resist belittling one another for our God-ordained distinctions. They enrich our lives. They are "the rest of the story." And in our Creator's words, it is "good."

My "helpmate suitable" suits me just fine.

A Man Faces Himself

1. Have some fun with your wife by taking turns asking each other questions such as: "If I had a millions dollars, I'd immediately _____." Or, "If I could spend one day doing anything I want, I would _____." Note the difference in your responses. Enjoy talking through any of those differences that may relate to male/female distinctions.

2. Ask your wife to name several (at least three) of the biggest differences between the way she sees the world and the way you see it. Give her a few days to think about it. Then take her to dinner and discuss her answers.

A Man Meets with His Friends

1. What do you think are the top five or six differences between men and women, other than anatomical differences?

2. Describe a time in your marriage when the differences between men and women caused a long-term, far-reaching problem.

3. Describe a time in your marriage when the differences between men and women brought about something delightful.

4. Do you agree that men are generally task-oriented, while women are generally people-oriented? Explain and illustrate your answer.

5. In what ways does our culture generally not accept differences between the sexes? How does this play out in your work place?

6. Talk through God's statement, "It is not good for the man to be alone." In what ways have you seen the truth of this statement?

7. Try to come up with several analogies similar to Gary Smalley's "buffalo and butterfly" scenario mentioned on pages 114 and 115. What other images fit the differences between men and women?

Does Anyone Here Speak 'Woman'?:

A Man and His Lady, Part 2

Love is to a man a thing apart...
'tis a woman's whole existence.
LORD BYRON

A S PASTOR OF a large church, I often receive a number of notes in the course of a week. Most are warm and encouraging. A few are... *less* warm and encouraging. To be honest, I probably need both, just to keep me on my toes—or my knees. Just recently however, I opened a note from a woman in our congregation that made me sit back in my chair.

I wasn't prepared for the depth of emotion. I wasn't prepared for twenty years of desolation distilled into twelve lines of neat, feminine cursive. She wrote it in the form of a poem, calling it, "Life in a Tomb."

> The emptiness of 20+ years.
> > The loss of hope.
> > The battle for joy with a good man
> > > a man content to be alone
> > > (but he needs me to be the keeper of his house,
> > > the mother of his children)
> > > a companion but no communion.

How can one endure contented
    with so little
        amidst so much material?
I worry for my soul
    living without love.

We're not living together very well as men and women. Relational despair has become a way of life in our culture. A popular family restaurant in Portland recently included this statement in one of its ads: "We'll cater for your weddings, for your rehearsal dinners, for your showers, your anniversaries, your birthdays, and your divorces." To our society's blurred and perverted way of thinking, separation and divorce have become a "natural" part of the flow of life. The unthinkable has become not only "thinkable," but the expected thing.

In 1912 there was only one divorce for every twelve marriages. By 1932 it had doubled to one for every six. By 1990 it was one for every two nationwide. In some areas of the nation it was even larger than that. And many of those who remain married, such as the woman who poured out her soul in that little poem, hang on to hope and sanity through the years by the thinnest of threads.

That's a problem of both women and men, of course, but I firmly believe that men bear a primary responsibility for this sorrow between the sexes. I agree with Dr. Richard Halverson, Chaplain of the United States Senate, who after sixty-nine years of life and forty-two years of marriage wrote:

> It is my deep, settled conviction that *one hundred percent* of the responsibility for the sustenance of the marriage relationship belongs to the husband. The scriptures tell us that as husbands we need to model ourselves after Jesus Christ, who gave Himself up in every way in order to present His bride to Himself without blemish or stain or spot or wrinkle.[1]

Someone has said, "Getting married is easy. Staying married is difficult. Staying happily married for a lifetime would be considered among the fine arts."

A Woman's Language

A fine art, yes. You might even call it a *language art*. Why? Because—let's get it on the table—women speak a different language than men. It's not Spanish or Korean or Swahili. It's not Hindi or Hebrew. It's "Woman," and it's spoken all over the planet. Yes, I suppose men have a language of sorts, too, but that's not the issue here. The crux of the matter is that women speak their own unique dialect and it is incumbent upon Tender Warriors to learn that language and speak it with passion.

I'm reminded of a cross-cultural snapshot one of my friends described to me. On a brief trip to Haiti, he found himself alone in a room with a young Haitian man who seemed wide-eyed with excitement about meeting an American. The Haitian obviously *longed* to open a conversation. His hands opened and closed. His eyes burned with a desire to weave his thoughts into understandable words. He seemed to have a thousand questions on the tip of his tongue. But my friend didn't speak a word of Creole and the Haitian didn't speak English. So eventually, after a few smiles, nods, vague gestures, and self-conscious shrugs, the two young men strolled awkwardly to different corners of the room, and then parted—almost certainly for the rest of their lives.

That little experience paints a powerful analogy in my mind. You and I know men and women who live together ten, twenty, *fifty* years or more but never learn to speak one another's language. They sit in rooms together, ride in cars together, eat meals together, take vacations together, and sleep together when the sun goes down. But for year after empty year they never learn how to get beyond vague gestures and a few surface phrases.

That, my friend, is a *man's* responsibility. He is the one who must take the initiative and learn how to speak "Woman." He is the one who must weather the awkward stuttering of lines from a woman's phrase book. So many give up after a few faltering, self-conscious attempts. *But real men don't have that option.* Real men "remain under" the responsibility, absorb the setbacks, swallow their pride, and keep trying. Real men stay and stay and stay.

When a man takes the risk and the initiative to learn his wife's language and understand her deepest needs, he is living out the heart of masculinity. Remember the ancient Hebrew words for man and woman—"piercer" and "pierced." It's up to the husband to take the initiative, to open up his wife's heart, to speak her language, to penetrate her world. And as we mentioned earlier, sexual relations represent only the tiniest portion of that huge reality. The physical is merely a parable of the spiritual.

He is an initiator and she is a responder. That's masculinity and femininity in the proverbial nutshell.

Simon Peter, the big fisherman, was a husband as well as an apostle of Jesus Christ. As an older man, he penned some words for his fellow husbands to wrestle with for the next couple millennia. Bear in mind that it is more than a bit of brotherly advice; it's the Word of God, a clear command of Scripture.

> You husbands…live with your wives in an understanding way, as with a weaker vessel, since she is a woman; and grant her honor as a fellow heir of the grace of life (1 Peter 3:7).

Let's zoom in on two pivotal phrases in that biblical imperative; two introductory lessons in learning to speak "Woman."

"Live with your wife in an understanding way…"

I once heard about a Swiss psychologist who spent his entire professional life studying the psychology of women. After more than thirty years on the job, he reportedly blurted out in a moment of frustration, *"What is it they want, anyway?"*

Apocryphal or real, the story represents what many men would admit to—moments of frustration trying to "figure out" their feminine friends. Many men have asked, "What is it they want, anyway?"

Is that question insulting to women? If you think about it for a moment, it ought to be an insult to men! Thirty years, and he couldn't figure it out? Where was his brain? Where is mine? Yours?

That's essentially what the apostle is saying here. "Men, live with your wives in an *understanding* way." In other words, "Men, engage your mind. Use that spherical object on your shoulders to live intelligently with this magnificent creature God has placed at your side."

Webster defines understanding as "gaining a full mental grasp." Not bad. Those are words we men ought to be able to grapple with. To understand is to gain a full mental grasp of the nature and significance of something. To understand is a mental process of arriving at a result. It's when you study and study an issue, turn it this way and that, and suddenly the wires connect, the light blinks on and you say, "Ah-ha! So *that's* the way it works!" There ought to be ah-ha's as we seek to comprehend the implications of womanhood. Men are commanded to understand, to comprehend, to apprehend the meaning of, to grasp the force of living with a woman. Understanding involves a discerning skill, a rational process, and a reasoned judgment.

Let me ask you this question: What would your business look like if you applied the same amount of mental and emotional energy to it that you do to understanding your wife? Am I far off the mark when I say that most of America would be bankrupt?

Use your head, men. Think it through. Work hard at it. Don't give up. *Understand.* Become a student of your wife and live in light of that knowledge.

"As with a weaker vessel..."

"Live with your wife in an understanding way as with a *weaker* vessel." What does Peter mean by "weaker"? You cannot use this verse or any other verse in scripture to teach male superiority or female inferiority. Not by a long shot. Peter is saying that a woman is weaker, not lesser.

But weaker in what sense? Certainly nobody objects to understanding a difference in physical brute strength. Even in this day of enforced gender quotas, you don't see too many women trying out for linebacker for the Dallas Cowboys or climbing into the ring to take on the heavyweight boxing champion. But he also means some other things. A woman is more delicate. She is the fine China, not the stoneware. She is a finely-tuned sports car, not a '66 Chevy pickup with mud flaps. She is more fragile, more sensitive. She has a more precisely adjusted sensory ability, especially in terms of relationships. A woman is more alert to what is happening in her environment. We men need to grasp the significance of these realities and *live with them wisely.*

That's what Peter means in this "weaker vessel" passage. Woman is a magnificent creature who by design requires provision and protection and care. It's not inferiority or superiority any more than blue is superior to green or green is inferior to blue or water is superior to air or air is superior to water. Men and women are profoundly *different...*by the Creator's own wise blueprint.

A Woman's Chemistry

As a man who seeks to apply intelligence to understanding my wife, I need to grapple with some facts of chemistry. The whole universe runs on chemistry. Have you ever thought about that? As you sit reading this book, you are a collection of chemicals. Yes, God made you with a spirit and a soul which are so much larger than your physical ingredients; but your chemistry does affect how you live. A woman was created with a vastly different chemistry from her counterpart. As men, we need to be attentive to that fact of life and sensitive to its implications.

Dr. James Dobson writes:

How can anyone who understands the cyclical pattern contend that there are no genetically determined psychological differences between males and females? No such system operates in men. The effect of the menstrual cycle is not only observed clinically, but it can be documented statistically. The incidences of suicides, homicides and infanticides perpetrated by women are significantly higher during the period of premenstrual tension than any other phase of the month.[2]

Men, get your eyes open. Get your brain engaged. Understand these things. Don't put her down for the way she was created! Understand her as delicate and fragile and alert and sensitive. Dobson goes on:

Consider also the findings of Alec Coppen and Neal Kessel, who studied 465 women and observed that they were more irritable and depressed during the premenstrual phase than during the mid-cycle. "This was true for neurotic, psychotic and normal women alike...." I receive interesting letters from men who ask, "How can I cope with my wife's irritability during this phase?"

Their question reminds me of an incident shared with me by my late friend, Dr. David Hernandez who was an obstetrician and gynecologist in private practice. The true story involves Latin men whose wives were given birth control pills by a pharmaceutical company. The Federal Drug Administration in America wouldn't permit hormonal research to be conducted, so the company selected a small fishing village in South America which agreed to cooperate. All the women in the town were given the pill on the same date, and after three weeks the prescription was terminated to permit menstruation. That meant, of course, that every adult female in the community was experiencing premenstrual tension at the same time. The men couldn't take it. They all headed for their boats each month and remained at sea until the crisis passed at home. They knew, even if some people didn't, that females are different from males...especially every 28 days.[3]

Women's Needs Are Different

It's chemistry, pure and simple. And that's only one factor in the gender equation. Men and women communicate in an utterly different way. Men and women *view life* in an utterly different way. Clinical psychologist and family therapist Dr. Willard Harley writes: "A man can have the best intentions to meet his wife's needs, but if he thinks her needs are similar to his own, he will fail miserably."[4]

A male writer in the *Arkansas Democrat* illustrates that point:

Women are very touchy about certain gifts, as I discovered years ago after buying my girlfriend a catcher's mitt for her birthday. It seemed to me to be a particularly thoughtful gift, especially since she claimed to not be getting enough exercise. But apparently, she didn't see it that way. The minute she unwrapped it, she ran sobbing from the room. At first I thought those were tears of joy streaming down her face. I figured she was overwhelmed at being the first in her crowd to have a catcher's mitt, that sort of thing. Or I figured she was so excited, she couldn't wait to get outside and work on her throws to second base. But when she didn't return after a few hours, I got the hint. Here I'd spent all that time running around from one sporting goods store to the next just to find the perfect gift—we're talking a Johnny Bench model here—top of the line, and she calls me "insensitive." I mean you'd think I gave her a year's subscription to *Field & Stream.* Or a box of shotgun shells, which everybody knows should be saved for Christmas stocking stuffers. Personally, I think she just had a lot of anger in her and took it out on me, not that I'm trying to play amateur psychologist or anything.[5]

This guy just wasn't getting it, was he? He wasn't understanding. Of course, it's a humorous newspaper column, but it's only funny because it's so close to reality. He obviously wasn't speaking her language—and didn't seem all that anxious to learn her needs.

So what are a woman's needs? What are the prerequisites for learning this wonderful, sometimes-bewildering language called "Woman"? Dr. Harley isolates five. The first is her need for *affection,* that is, tenderness. The second is *conversation,* the sharing of the heart. The third is *honesty and openness;* no secrets between us. The fourth is *security,* or physical and financial provision. The fifth is *relational commitment.* She must know she is a priority.

Scripture refines those five feminine needs down into three imperatives for men: *honor, nourish, cherish.*

And listen friends, that's no academic exercise—*it's an action plan.* Shakespeare said it this way, "They do not love that do not show their love." That's what was happening in the home of the woman who wrote the poem about living in a tomb. I know her husband, and he *is* a good man. He has the best of intentions. He does love his wife. He just doesn't know how to say it or show it. He never effectively learned his wife's language.

Olivia Newton John, that other great English lyricist, stated it a little more bluntly when she sang, "If you love me let me know; if you don't then let me go."

That's it. You have to show it. Love has to be demonstrated. Verbalized. Expressed. Woven into real words and real deeds. How does a man love a woman? He learns to know her needs and consistently speaks her language in meeting them.

Learning the Lingo

I can testify that at least one hospital in Portland, Oregon, knows the difference between men's and women's needs. When I had back surgery in this hospital, I can remember them wheeling me back into my room. It had all the standard furnishings: a bed, a night stand, white walls, and a tiny digital clock. That was about it for decor. You know...Basic Alcatraz. Once in a while they'd bundle me down the hall to a phone-booth sized chamber where I'd climb into a stainless steel drum for hydrotherapy.

Then my wife had surgery in the same hospital, followed by a short stay on the women's ward. Have you ever been in a women's ward? It has *wallpaper*. Everywhere. And curtains. And matching "dusty rose" bedspreads. She had a fancy designer clock in her room, and a gorgeous Ethan Allen chair in the corner. I thought I was in the Ritz-Carlton. And instead of a steel washtub in a phone booth, the nurse came in and cooed, "Gooood morning, sweetheart. Would we like our jacuzzi now?" I got a peek at that jacuzzi room. It was tiled, floor to ceiling, with fancy floral patterns.

Everything about the surroundings said, "We speak a woman's language. We care. We honor you. We cherish you. We nourish you here." Yes, it's a different vernacular than most men are accustomed to. But don't despair, gentlemen. You can learn that lingo. And you don't need a fancy jacuzzi or floral tile to do it. *You can speak the language of demonstrative love in a way that your wife understands.* All it takes is a little forethought, a willingness to stretch the edges of your comfort zone, and a rock-hard commitment to stick with it.

Let me cite a few examples. In my estimation, greeting cards are one of the greatest forms of corporate larceny in America. They cost so much and they say so little. They're not even all that attractive, in my estimation—unless they have dogs or ducks or boats on 'em. But to a woman's way of thinking, a card means everything.

You want another example? A cut flower is an incredible waste of money. I mean, it's *dead*, isn't it? It's already fading and decaying before you get it paid for. And what does it do? What's it good for? But in a woman's language, it somehow speaks volumes.

Several years ago I was on my way to the hospital to make a pastoral call. As I passed the shopping mall where Linda worked, something strange came over me. It must have been supernatural; it was certainly out of the ordinary for me. I stopped at a grocery store that has flowers in a refrigerator. I bought a little flower in a bud vase, drove to the mall parking lot, and found Linda's car. I have a key to her car, so I opened the door and set the little vase with a little card between the seats. Then I locked up the car and went on to the hospital.

That night at home as we were talking about it, I asked, "What did you think when you first saw the flower?"

"I knew somebody had been in my car,"she replied. (Implication: It couldn't have been *you*.) After checking the back seat to make sure no one was hiding there, she sat in the car and opened up the card. And wept.

My wife cried for joy over a card which maybe cost a buck, and a little flower which maybe cost three or four. But it *spoke* to her. It said, "I'm harboring you in my mind. I'm understanding who you are as a woman." For five or six dollars, I actually spoke a few simple words in her language. And guys...she heard me loud and clear.

Another time one of my friends and I tried something wildly out of character for both of us. We realized we might end up making fools of ourselves trying to speak an unfamiliar language, but we sucked it up and said, "Hey, life is short. This thing might fall through, but let's give it a shot."

Roger has a little piece of property on a hilltop that looks out over some mountains and a beautiful little valley. So we decided to have a fancy surprise picnic for our wives. First we had to go up on the hilltop and mow a section of waist-high wild grass. With my hay fever, it about killed me. My eyes nearly swelled shut. But a man stays at a task, right? We got it done. Then we hauled a table and chairs up there. We draped the table with a white table cloth and put a pretty candelabra in the middle of it.

At a nearby deli, we found some really nice stuff to eat and sparkling cider and that kind of thing. Then we got our girls (who were wondering what we were up to) and took them up on that hill.

That was many years ago. But Linda still remembers and relishes that day. She'll never forget it. It wasn't just the picnic or hauling stuff up a hillside that moved her heart. It was the fact that I would go to all that trouble to speak her language.

Though I'm not especially good at this kind of thing, I do remember another attempt several years ago. When it works out, I try to take Fridays off. At the time, Linda worked in a department store and got off at noon. I was sitting there reading the paper that morning and thought, *Hey, I could do for her what she's always doing for me. I'll fix lunch.* Now if you really want to be speaking the language, you don't eat lunch at the regular table in the kitchen. When a woman wants to express special care, she serves the meal at the "nice" table in the dining room. Admittedly, it doesn't make a lot of sense. You have to haul the food farther and clean up the big table. But that's what she does, so that's what I was going to do, since I was trying to speak her language.

I got out the china and the crystal and set them up on the far ends of the table like they do in the old movies. It looked really good, but now came the big challenge. What was I going to put *on* the china? I don't cook at all. I mean zero. When I go hunting, I live off of dough-nut holes and milk. But I had to put something on those plates, because it looked lonely out there on the table. Then I remembered something Linda occasionally does on Sunday nights. She takes an English muffin, cuts it in half, and fixes a little tuna thing.

I did that, but now it looked *really* lonely. A pile of tuna on a tiny muffin, all by itself on a great big white plate. Then it came back to me how Linda would sometimes melt cheese over the tuna and stick little pieces of pineapple in it. So I did that. It didn't look too bad. Then I put some red punch in the crystal and stood back to survey my work. Honestly, it looked pretty classy. Okay, it wasn't *Better Homes & Gardens,* but it wasn't too tacky, either.

Then she came in the door. You would have thought I'd just bought the Queen Mary and announced that we were going on a year's cruise. She was absolutely blown away. All I said was, "Hi, honey," but in her language, I'd just recited a Shakespearean sonnet accompanied by a mandolin. I wasn't only speaking "Woman," I was *singing*. That simple little effort (for pity's sake, it was only *tuna fish*) communicated in a way that was all out of proportion to the act itself.

The RESPONDER portion of a woman's soul is so strong! It seems to take even the most feeble effort of masculine tenderness and reflect it back in a blaze of feminine glory. When Linda responds with such joy and warmth it almost makes me ashamed at how seldom I exert myself in that direction. But the fact remains...when I as the lover and initiator attempt to speak her language and penetrate her world, she is all I've ever dreamed of as a woman in response to me.

Even Imperfect Attempts Are Welcome

Okay, so you feel inept at speaking "Woman." You feel like you'll say the wrong thing or buy the wrong size or wreck the tuna fish or botch it up somehow. But think about it for a minute. Would *you* be offended by someone who doesn't know English very well, but comes up to you and makes a real effort to greet you in a broken dialect? It may come out in a funny, halting way, but does that put you off? Does it insult you or make you turn away in disgust? Of course not. The attempt even endears this individual to you.

Years ago Linda and I had the opportunity to travel to Switzerland. While we were there, we took the time to look up some of my German-speaking relatives, separated from the American branch of the family for five generations when my great grandparents emigrated. It wasn't easy to locate them, and we had no idea what our reception would be. It could have been an embarrassment. It could have been a big-time cultural foul-up. When we finally found them, they spoke no English, and we could only stammer around in broken, high school German. But somehow it didn't matter. The camaraderie we experienced and the pleasure and sheer delight on their faces more than made up for the lack of precise terminology. The attempts—fumbling and stumbling as they may have been—only seemed to magnify our newfound kinship. What so moved them was that we had been willing to make the attempt. We had gone out of our way to find them and greet them and embrace them. They realized that if we had not gone to those lengths to say "You and I are kin," we would never have met.

Men, we need to make the effort, take the risk, and speak the language. A woman needs honoring and cherishing and nourishing. She needs to know she is the top priority in her man's life. In the early years of our marriage, I tended to look at my wife as my "partner." I sang bass, she sang soprano. I was playing right guard, she was playing tackle. She was my executive assistant. She was my fellow worker. She was my fellow soldier. She was my wing man. But a woman doesn't want to be a wing man. She doesn't want to be a tackle. She doesn't even want to be a junior "partner" in all your endeavors.

She wants to be in your heart and soul. She wants to hear it from you and see it in you.

Do you remember when your first child was born? Do you remember what that day felt like? Do you remember those emotions of tenderness you felt toward this lady who had just borne you that little son or daughter? I'll never forget it. I walked down the hallway in that hospital with my chest expanded about three shirt sizes, eyes alert for somebody to broadcast my story to. What I wanted to broadcast was, "Hey world, this is my wife, this is my *woman*, this is my miracle worker. Look what she has done!"

Do you remember that feeling? Well, *bottle it.* Bottle that feeling of pride and cherishing and treasuring and nourishing and honoring. And once you've bottled it, slap a liberal dose on both cheeks every morning.

Some of you by the providence of God have not been able to have those children. Your task is even more profound. You find that pride and put it on five times a day. Do battle with hell itself for the sake of your woman and your marriage. Polish the treasure where you live and forget the mythical one at the end of Hollywood's rainbow. All you need is under your own roof if you'll only acknowledge it and cherish it.

That's how to live with a woman. That's how to speak her language. Down through the long years it is an effort that will chase loneliness out of dark corners and paint joyful murals on the hallways of your life.

And it sure beats living in a tomb.

A Man Faces Himself

1. Are you ready for a challenge? Call up two or three of your wife's closest friends and ask *them* what "language" your wife speaks.

2. Identify, write down, and carry in your wallet, two ways apiece that you can honor, nourish, and cherish your wife in the next thirty days.

A Man Meets with His Friends

1. Do you agree with the statement, "we're not living very well together as men and women"? Explain your answer.

2. What "language" does your own wife speak? What difficulties have you experienced trying to understand it? What progress have you made in learning it? Have you really connected in some key areas?

3. Answer the question for yourself: "What would your business look like if you applied the same amount of mental and emotional energy to it that you do to understanding your wife?"

4. Have you caught a glimpse of Peter's meaning when he says your wife is a "weaker vessel"? How do you understand this term? How does it practically affect the way you relate to your wife?

5. This chapter cited five needs of every woman: affection, conversation, honesty and openness, security, and relational commitment. How are you doing with them? Which one gives you the most trouble? Why?

6. When was the last time you made a deliberate attempt to speak your wife's "language"? What was the result?

The Incredible Power of Fathering:

A Man and His Children, Part 1

He commanded our fathers, that they should teach...their children, that the generation to come might know, even the children yet to be born...[to] put their confidence in God and...keep His commandments
(PSALM 78:5-7).

WHAT IS THE MOST powerful word in the English language? Have you ever thought about it? List some possibilities. Love? Hope? Vision? Sacrifice? There are many candidates.

How about *Dad?*

Ever thought of it that way before? It's worth considering. Just walk through what you know about life. When it comes to power in a youngster's world, I'll put my money on "Dad." As words go, *hope, vision,* and *sacrifice* don't mean a whole lot to little tykes. But the power of "Dad" reaches far beyond a youngster's childhood. In fact, it spans *generations.*

There are two ways to recognize power. One is to see it at work. The other is to measure what happens when it is gone. Either way, "Dad" is pretty potent. Present or absent. Positive or negative. The power of a father is incredible.

We all long for our fathers. I feel the connection deeply in myself. I see it strongly in my sons. I observe it repeatedly as I counsel men and women in our church. I read about it in book after book. I see it dissected and examined in movie after movie. And in almost every person I know well—male or female—I observe the insatiable desire for an unbreakable, soulish bond to our fathers.

I remember years ago standing on the banks of the Yakima River, in central Washington. I was just a boy, and boys on river banks toss rocks. My dad was with me, and we were throwing rocks together. They would fly farther and farther out into the current with their tell-tale splashes. It was pretty exciting stuff to see just how far out into this swift, wide river we could wing those missiles.

Then something awesome happened. Dad picked up a rock a little larger than the others. He windmilled it once around his shoulder, stepped into it, and *heaved* that rock like I had not seen before. Wide-eyed, I traced its arc into the sky, watching it seemingly gather power as it flew. And it sailed clear across...all the...("holy jumpin' toledo!")...it cleared the whole river and bounced on the opposite bank. My jaw dropped. To this youngster it was an awe-inspiring display of raw power. My little mind couldn't put it all together. But I do remember wondering that day if my dad might really be Clark Kent. Superman. I thought to myself, *I am the son of the most powerful man in the universe.* Everything in me swelled up. I wanted to be just like him. I wanted to walk in my father's shoes.

Little did I know then that my father's impressive physical strength was just a metaphor of the incredible spiritual strength of a father. It was a visible symbol of an invisible reality. Like no other person, a father possesses a special power to mold another's life, shape it, give it form. Concepts of character flow from this man's life. Esteem. Principles. Identity. And anchor points. When you think about it awhile, there are few things more powerful.

An interview with Keith Meyering, administrator for Men's Life, illustrates the incredible spiritual power of a father in a child's life. He states:

> When the father is an active believer there is about a seventy-five percent likelihood that the children will also become active believers. But if only the mother is a believer this likelihood is dramatically reduced to fifteen percent.[1]

Fathering Is at the Heart of Masculinity

We've been asking the question in this book, "What is a man? What is at the heart of masculinity?" We saw a number of traits in the creation accounts of man, the headwaters. A man is responsible for pro-vision. He's to see ahead—spiritually, physically, mentally, and emotionally. That's the king in him, the royal blood of the provider. A man is a protector. A man is a teacher or mentor. A man is a care-giver, a friend.

Now how would you summarize those four pillars of masculinity —King, Warrior, Mentor, and Friend? If you could picture one word that you could just drop over the top of those basic tenets of man-hood, what would it be? What one word would you pick to describe the heart of masculinity?

Again, it's *Dad*, isn't it? *Father*.

What a word. What a power-packed word. Is it any wonder all of God's children are taught to pray, "Our Father, who art in heaven..."

He is the ultimate King and Pro-visionary. He has seen ahead from eternity past.

He is the ultimate Protector and Warrior. He is the One who stands between us and the Evil One who would devour us.

He is the ultimate Mentor and Transformer. He is the Master Teacher whose law is truth and whose word sustains life.

He is the ultimate Friend. Care-giver. Lover. He gave everything He had—including His own Son—to care for us. There is no greater love.

And He loves to be called, "Abba, Father." Our Father God is the Ultimate King, Warrior, Mentor, and Friend. Perhaps His pre-eminence is the reason the concept of Father runs so deeply in all our hearts. He is... "*our* Father." He is the Father "from whom every family in heaven and on earth draws its name" (Ephesians 3:15). He is the Father of fathers. He is the reason we all long for our fathers. It must not be accidental then that the Old Testament closes with a look at the future and wraps up earth history in what I call "father terms."

See, I will send you the prophet Elijah before that great and dreadful day of the LORD comes. He will turn the hearts of the fathers to their children, and the hearts of the children to their fathers... (Malachi 4:5-6, NIV).

While I do not understand all that passage means, I do believe it is a significant statement of God's intention that human history be viewed in familial terms, that men—fathers—are critical to the Father's design, and that there will be no peace on this earth until men learn what it is to be a man...after God's heart.

Gordon Dalbey, a Christian author with a keen interest in men, takes it a step further:

The biblical faith understands that healing between fathers and children is not simply a psychological exercise to bring greater peace of mind; instead, it is the essential prerequisite to fulfilling God's purposes on earth. When fathers are reconciled with sons and daughters, God's saving power is released among us; conversely, when fathers and children remain at odds with one another, powers of destruction are beckoned.[2]

Our Culture Bears Out the Power of Fathering

Even a glance at our culture bears out the power of fathering...or the power of its absence. It may very well be that the major problems in America today stem from a lack of fatherhood. Economics. Politics. Poverty. Gender confusion. Urban gangs. Think about it. Fathering is so incredibly powerful that, like gravity—whether you recognize it or not, whether you believe in it or not, whether you think it touches you or not—it does indeed affect you. Like a gigantic magnetic field, it pulsates with power, energy, and effect.

Dr. James Dobson says, "Our very survival as a people will depend on the presence or absence of masculine leadership in millions of homes." Professor Max Lerner writes, "The 'vanishing father' is perhaps the central fact of the changing American family structure today." An article in the *New York Times Magazine* states, "The Youth Board realized it had penetrated into a world where there is no father. The welfare world of New York is a fatherless world." London's *Daily Telegraph* warns,

Entire neighborhoods will probably become dominated by an

underclass of young delinquents within the next decade. The scale of crime...violence, and drug taking could easily surpass that of American cities. The fewer fathers in a community, the more the children would run wild.[3]

Robert Bly, poet of the current men's movement, notes the pain of this fatherlessness:

Being lied to by older men amounts to a broken leg. When the young men arrived in Viet Nam and found they'd been lied to, they received immeasurably deep wounds. Never being welcomed into the male world by older men is a wound in the chest. The police chief of Detroit remarked that the young men he arrests not only don't have any responsible older man in the house, they have never met one. When you look at a gang, you're looking, as Michael Meade remarked, at young men who have no older men around them at all.[4]

How we long for our fathers! How powerfully we are affected by our fathers—present or absent, negative or positive. And it isn't just boys who feel both the waves and undertow of that vast force. Listen to this heart-wrenching letter I received from a dear woman in our congregation:

My dad was what I thought was a real man.... He was the provider and worked hard for our physical needs. He had to go 150 miles away from home to find work, coming home often only on weekends.... As could be expected, I didn't know my dad very well.

When I reached adolescence, I began to desire more than any-thing to win his approval...it became an all-consuming need. I went back and forth from being a tomboy to being feminine to try to get him to like me. I took up fishing and made myself pull worms apart and get slime underneath my finger-nails so that I could bait my own hooks and we could go fish-ing. But he didn't have time to go fishing anymore.

I started playing softball and became the best pitcher in our school. But he never saw me play a game. I worked hard to get straight A's and was always on the honor roll. Never once did he say he was proud of me.... One year I was a cheer-leader. He never came to a game. One year I was captain of the drill team. He never saw a performance.

One weekend I tried to help him work on the car. But he was cross with me and I was in the way. I went into the house and made some cookies. He said I baked them too long.

More and more I found myself retreating to my room on the weekends, sobbing violently, desperately wanting him to care. Not once did he comfort me. He never read to me. He never tucked me into bed. He never hugged me. He never kissed me. He never said, "I love you."

I got married and had four kids. The last one was a boy, the only male descendant. We gave him his name. He wasn't impressed. Restless and dissatisfied with mothering, I went back to school.

Somehow, without meaning to, I found myself studying civil engineering, the field of study closest to his profession. I worked as a surveyor last year laying out lines just like the lines he had put in for years. I found myself thinking, "If he could see me now, he would be proud of me."

What a power a father has over the direction of a daughter's life. Good or bad, present or absent, he is going to have an influence that lasts a lifetime. I think a lot of fathers leave their daughters to the mothers to raise, thinking a man's influence isn't necessary for girls.

I'm thirty-seven years old now and beginning to see how much I am still compelled by a deep craving within to gain the approval of this most significant man. You see, if my own father doesn't think I'm worthwhile, I must be worthless. If my own father can't accept me, then I am unacceptable. If my own father cannot love me, then I must be totally unlovable. If I'm truly worthless and unacceptable and unlovable, then God couldn't really love me. And certainly my dear husband, who is only human, couldn't really love me.

I thank God that He's opening my eyes to these lies and showing me His truth. He has begun the process of healing, but the wounds are really deep. I fear the affects of the scarring will be with me while I remain on this earth.

They probably will. And they will likely touch those four kids, too. And their kids. That's the incredible power of fathering. It extends transgenerationally to the third and fourth generations.

My own wife knows the pain of an abusive father who eventually abandoned the family completely when she was fifteen years old. Experiencing those scars, she determined she'd do everything in her power to see that her own children never went through it (not that I ever intended to go anywhere, of course).

So when Uncle Sam sent me orders to Vietnam, she took action. Determined to minimize my absence for Kent, our infant son, she went to the local bookstore and bought two copies of each key childhood storybook we thought Kent would enjoy. I took one to Vietnam, and she kept one here. I read the stories to him from across the Pacific via small tapes I sent home. She sat Kent on her lap, played the tapes of my voice reading the stories, and turned the pages of the books for Kent, keeping pace with my voice. No child of hers was going to lose touch with his father if she had anything to do with it. Even Uncle Sam couldn't interrupt story time.

What Do You Remember about Your Father?

Think back through your own memories. Work with them. Where they're negative, get help. Seek counsel. Where they're positive, reproduce them. Pass them on.

I remember my dad's hairy arms. I always wanted hairy arms, like Dad. Silly? No, just a childhood fascination with the nature of masculine maturity in the physical realm, the easiest one for a child to see. I wanted to be like him. And if that meant hairy arms, I couldn't wait.

I remember my dad's body odor. Sound peculiar? Maybe. But you probably do, too. I remember thinking in my little-boy-like way, "I wonder if I'll smell like that someday." I remember thinking that maybe that was the special scent of our clan, the tribal distinctive, so to speak. We didn't wear some of the ancient family-tribal markings I had seen on TV or in *National Geographic*. Maybe this was our way. I wanted to grow up into that someday.

I wanted to pray like my dad prayed. I wanted to understand the Bible the way he understood the Bible. I wanted to grapple with the mystery of "God's Plan of the Ages," like he always talked about in that grand, admiring tone of voice. I wanted to take hold of life the same way he took hold of life.

Why aren't more men "taking hold" in our country? Why aren't more men showing young hands where to "hold on"? Could it be that the Industrial Revolution and its aftermath took Dad out of the home entirely? Have we therefore forgotten what dads do? What real men are all about?

Our culture is out of step. We are out of order. And there's nothing more painful to witness than men who have forgotten what a man is. Dr. Henry Biller speaks a mouthful when he says:

> The principal danger to fatherhood today is that fathers do not have the vital sense of father power that they have had in the past. Because of a host of pressures from society, the father has lost the confidence that he is naturally important to his children, that he has the power to affect children, to guide them and help them grow. He isn't confident that fatherhood is a basic part of being masculine and the legitimate focus of his life."[5]

At the root of masculinity is fatherhood. But think of that term in large, rather than narrow terms. If you don't have children of your own, you can still father. Fathering is a vast field. The easiest aspect of fatherhood is the most obvious and physical—reproducing children biologically. But fathering has only a little to do with biology. At its heart it has everything to do with originating, influencing, and shaping. I believe if we understand it rightly, we will conclude that every man is, at his soul level, a father (king, warrior, teacher, friend), whether he has biological children or not.

"Boys become men by watching men, by standing close to men. Manhood is a ritual passed from generation to generation with precious few spoken instructions. Passing the torch of manhood is a fragile, tedious task. If the rite of passage is successfully completed, the boy-become-man is like an oak of hardwood character. His shade and influence will bless all those who are fortunate enough to lean on him and rest under his canopy."

PRESTON GILLHAM
from "Lifetime Guarantee"

Begin with the Dictionary

Father. Look the word right in the eye. Webster is straightforward: "One who has begotten a child; one who cares for; one to whom respect is due; an originator; a source."

Personally, I believe father has more to do with the "caring" than the "begetting." Begetting can take place in a thoughtless moment of passion. Fathering never will. Begetting can be utterly selfish. Fathering never can.

Father. Its verb form is even more strikingly potent—"To beget. To be a founder. To be the foundation. To author." Think through the implications of that verb—*father*—in your home, workplace, or in the affairs of daily living. To *father* is to be the one who puts together the scope and sequence of life. To be the one who authors and creates the curriculum for the development of generations to come. To be the author. To accept responsibility for.

To take hold! To grip groping young hands with tender strength and hold on until young feet have confidence on the sometimes-dark, sometimes-slippery path.

My dad's physical strength showed up a lot in projects, chores, and things such as throwing rocks across rivers. But on one day in particular, I was struck again with that strength and how it could touch me.

Down the hill from our house was a vacant lot. On one occasion Dad and I were down there together...must have been playing catch, I don't remember. But I'll never forget the run up the hill.

In the midst of our activity, Mom came to the front porch of "old 3309" (an affectionate reference to our home) and called us to dinner. Dad and I glanced at each other. Our eyes met. They sparkled. Without a word we both sensed it was "time for a race." We took off. It was about 150 yards uphill to the house. It was glorious running along with my dad. Man, it was great! But try as I might, my little legs couldn't keep up with his long ones. He started to pull ahead. My neck strained. My muscles stretched. But I was losing ground. Then something really special happened.

Dad, seeing me start to drop back, reached out his hand to me.

His eyes said, *Grab hold. Let's run together.*

Still running, my little hand slipped inside his larger one. It was like magic! His power lifted me right off the ground. I took off in his strength. My speed doubled because my dad had hold of me.

That's a lot like life. A kid's speed doubles when dad takes hold at home. *Take hold,* Dad! Hold on for all you're worth. Hold on in the face of storms and disappointments and sorrows and temptations and hurts and crazy, churning circumstances. There isn't much of anything in life children can't face with Dad's strong hand wrapped tightly around theirs.

And while you're at it, with your other hand, hold on tightly to your heavenly Father's hand. Let Him be your confidence and wisdom and stability when you just can't find your own. Let His strength pull you up life's long hills until you stand together, laughing and catching your breath, on heaven's front porch.

Isn't that what dads are for?

A Man Faces Himself

1. Ever wonder what your children might say to a newspaper reporter interviewing them about their dad...after your death? Imagine that *you* are that reporter. Take thirty minutes and write your own obituary from the perspective of your kids. It'll be sobering, encouraging, and instructive. And it could make a huge difference in your actual obituary. Do it.

2. Try keeping a journal for one week, recording how much time you spend and how much insight you gain cultivating your relationship with God, the ultimate father.

A Man Meets with His Friends

1. What do you think of when you hear the word "dad"?

2. How has your relationship with your own dad affected the way you live today?

3. Take a look around your neighborhood. How has the presence or absence of strong fathers shaped your community?

4. Re-read the quote from Dr. Henry Biller on page 138. Do you agree or disagree? Why?

5. How have you "taken hold" of your own children in order to inspire confidence in them? How can you improve your "hold"?

6. Are you "taking hold" of your heavenly Father's hand? What does this mean, in practical terms?

CHAPTER TEN

Spanning the Generations:

A Man and His Children, Part 2

The glory of sons is their fathers
(PROVERBS 17:6).

THE POWER OF fathering rolls like an irresistible undercurrent through the pages of Scripture. From beginning to end. From Genesis to Revelation. From Eden to Armageddon. Sometimes it's underground, a muted thunder beneath the feet, a barely discernible vibration in the chest cavity. At other times it bursts to the surface in a majestic torrent, carving mighty canyons in the biblical landscape.

It is clearly implied in the ancient covenants.

God is a promise maker and keeper—a very "fatherly trait," wouldn't you say? All of the Bible and human history hinge on His promises. We call them "covenants." The most basic of these is the Abrahamic covenant. It governs all the subsequent covenants. Abram had no children. God determined to give him some—lots! At the giving of that covenant, God changed his name from Abram to Abraham, the latter meaning "the father of nations." In Genesis 17, 18, and 19 when that covenant is ratified, God says "I will make you the father of a multitude of nations." Further, the Lord says, "I have chosen him in order that he may command his children and his household after him to keep the way of the Lord by doing righteousness and justice."

Notice something? Who was chosen to command? What is the gender of the pronouns in that passage? Masculine, of course. Have you ever noticed that in the giving of those promises upon which history hangs, God did not address Sarah? Was that because He thought less of her? That He somehow overlooked her or minimized her person and her role? Of course not. God valued Sarah equally. But equality is not sameness. Remember, value is not function. Sarah was given a different function than her husband. God gave fatherhood to the male. To the man. Not because he was any better, but just because He chose to do so. He wanted to do it that way. And when you're God, you get to call the shots. We would all do well to figure out His system and get on the right side of it. As a man, I am responsible for the development of our children. God did not leave it to my wife. Neither can I. Dad is responsible.

It is implied in the powerful vision of the psalmist.

For he established a testimony in Jacob, and appointed a law in Israel, which He commanded our fathers, that they should teach them to their children, that the generation to come might know, even the children yet to be born, that they may arise and tell them to their children (Psalm 78:5-6).

Fatherhood is transgenerational in its power. That was the vision of the psalmist. We'll focus on that thought in a moment or two.

It was the wonderful hope of the prophets.

I will send you the prophet Elijah before that great and dreadful day of the LORD comes. He will turn the hearts of the fathers to their children, and the hearts of the children to their fathers" (Malachi 4:5-6, NIV).

Malachi is saying, in essence, that when this world is at last put in order, when heaven on earth is realized at last, when God the Father's intentions are all put together and realized, it will look like family with Dad in his proper role.

It is the simple command of the New Testament.

"Fathers," Paul exhorts, "bring [your children] up in the discipline and instruction of the Lord" (Ephesians 6:4). No mention of mothers there. Not that they don't bring their children up. But the responsibility for it rests with Dad. And dads are cautioned to be careful how they do it: "Do not provoke your children to wrath." Don't ever abuse your father power. It's just too potent to misuse. It would be like playing football with a freezer bag full of nitroglycerin. Sooner or later it will explode and maim and disfigure. We will answer to the Ultimate Father for our use of His delegated power.

The great river of fathering that leaped from the primordial mists of Eden rolls through time and into eternity. How will you bend the course of the tributary that flows in your family? You *will* affect it, you know. For good or ill. Whether you work at it with all your heart and soul or close your eyes and ears and put your hands in your pockets and pretend it doesn't exist, you will channel that river in one direction or another. That's the nature of fathering. You can't hide from its potency and power. Whether you like it or not, whether you accept it or not, whether you *believe* it or not, your influence will span generations long after you've left this earth.

Remember the founders of this nation? We've called them pilgrims. The leaders of that group of pilgrims were men who I believe understood manhood. And fathering. They were confident of the power of fathering. They wanted their families, the generations to come, to grow up "in the nurture and admonition of the Lord." They knew that was where life was sourced. And since it couldn't easily happen where they had lived previously, they left—pilgrims. To father a new way of life. To lay a foundation. To take responsibility for future generations. That was fathering at its finest. Truly, they are our fathers, even though most of us are unrelated to them biologically. They were truly patriots—a word drawn from the root word for father. And for all of our politically correct "multi-cultural" rejection of this heritage, the canyons and valleys and mountain peaks of our nation still echo the song of the pilgrim fathers. The best of who we are can be traced back to their godly fathering at the dawn of our nationhood.

That is the incredible power of fathering. It is so potent it is *trans-generational* in scope. Both positive and negative. For example, the Bible indicates that the sins of the fathers extend "to the third and fourth generation" (Exodus 34:7). Like a great pulsating magnetic field, father power is so strong it will outlive every father who reads these pages. Psychologists examine the "family of origin" for this reason. Therapists trace "dysfunctions" through a family for generations.

The power of fathering is so intrinsically wrapped up in the nature of God—the ultimate father—that the world of nature sees its influence rolling on and on and on for *generations*. God the Father has so woven His own nature into the warp and woof of His universe that it is inviolable. There is something so inherently strong, so deep, so profound, and so natural in fathering, that father power is visibly transgenerational in its potency. You can *see* it. Good, bad, or indifferent, it lives on. Fatherhood is so powerful that it outlives even itself.

A Father, Son, and Grandpa, Too

You will be felt down through the generations. That is true not only physically or genetically, but spiritually and psychologically as well. Those who have never seen my grandfather, William Weber, need only take a look at my son Blake Weber. He's his "spittin' image."

That picture of Grandpa in his Navy uniform, taken in 1908, looks like it could have been snapped of Blake in 1993. And Grandpa's character is still walking the streets today in a number of his great-grandchildren.

We have all long acknowledged the genetic similarities to our "forefathers," but we are only beginning to wake up to the incredible psychological, or "soulish" similarities. And they are the more important. Blake bears the *spiritual* imprint of his great-grandfather even more clearly than he does his physical imprint. And there are obvious parallels in character traits, too. William loved people. So does Blake. Little kids flocked around Grandpa (he always had candy in his pockets and Pepsi in his fridge). They follow Blake the same way. William had a mischievous sense of humor. Blake, too.

Blake never met his great-grandfather. We buried Grandpa the same year Blake was born. We have just one four-generation picture, and that includes only our firstborn, Kent. The picture was taken in a nursing home when Grandpa was in his late eighties. Life had been hard for him during his final years. Requiring increasing amounts of technical health care, Grandpa eventually had to make his way to a nursing home. But William Weber just wasn't a man cut out for a nursing home, if you know what I mean. He'd worked hard all his life. He was a coal miner. He cleared land...whatever it took to provide a little food, a little shelter, and a lot o' togetherness.

His body had finally let him down. He was thin and bedridden. Didn't look much like Grandpa anymore. Didn't act much like him, either. Being confined to bed had taken its toll on his spirit, and he was a little apathetic, something he'd never been a day in his life.

But then Linda and I came home from an army assignment in Europe. I could hardly wait to introduce Grandpa to his first great-grandchild. Eight months old, Kent could perhaps add a little life to Grandpa's day. Or so I had hoped.

I was not prepared for what was to take place.

I walked into Grandpa's room, holding my son in my arms. Speaking in a louder than normal "nursing home voice," I introduced him to his little descendant. Grandpa came up off that bed! The pillow couldn't hold him anymore. His eyes literally lit up. Linda captured that moment on film. Four generations. Dad at the head of the bed. Me beside him. Kent in my arms. And our frail little patriarch with bright eyes and outstretched arms literally coming up out of those sheets full of joy.

You've never met William Joseph Weber, either. Let me tell you a little bit about him. Orphaned at an early age, he spent some time in the Boys and Girls Aid Society of New York. After a few years in the orphanage, at about age nine he was placed on one of the "orphan trains" and shipped to the Midwest. Maybe he misunderstood, maybe it was real, but he always felt that farmers sort of "bought" the kids off the train at different stops along the way. He felt the treatment he was given and the farm work he was required to perform sounded about as close as he'd ever want to come to slave labor. He lasted on his adopted farm for a few years, ran away, and ended up as a teen in the back of a cobbler's shop, sleeping on a cot. Before long he ran away from there, lied about his age, and joined the Navy. He traveled around the world in Teddy Roosevelt's Great White Fleet.

What's my point? He never knew a father. He barely knew a mother before she died. He never knew a family or a real, permanent home. He never experienced any of the things we normally consider healthy in a "family of origin."

But somewhere along the line, he found Jesus Christ.

He determined to put his "confidence in God...and keep his commandments" (Psalm 78:7). No, he never knew his own father. But he pursued the ultimate Father. Reading wasn't easy for him, but he did it. Of all the books in my library today, my favorite is one of his—a worn, broken old copy of Matthew Henry's Commentary on the New Testament. You can still find traces of his fingerprints there from the coal dust on his hands.

My grandfather pursued the Father.

His son, Byron, did too. So did the grandchildren. And the great-grandchildren. He left us quite a heritage. He changed his world. And right now our world desperately needs you and me to do the same.

No, you've never met William Joseph Weber, but there is a strong possibility he is affecting you now as you turn the pages of this book. Most Sundays, he affects the folks who gather in our church and hear me preach. He was my Grandpa. What I am, I owe to him and his son, my father. In fact, I'm in the ministry today due largely to their influence. The spiritual heritage that awakened within me in the Dak Poko Valley was his. He encouraged me toward the ministry.

I'll never forget the time I preached my first message. I was seventeen years old. It was in a little Nazarene church in the backwoods of central Washington. Grandpa and Grandma, with one other couple, had started the church years before. There must have been all of a dozen people seated there on that Sunday. But as I looked down at the front row, I'll never forget the sparkle in Grandpa's eyes. It was the same one I would see years later in the nursing home. I've forgotten the message I preached there in that little country church. But I will never forget the message I *received* there.

Oh, the power of fathering—and grandfathering—is incredible.

"An almost perfect relationship with his father was the earthly root of all his wisdom. From his own father, he said, he first learned that fatherhood must be at the core of the universe. He was thus prepared in an unusual way to teach that religion in which the relation of father and son is of all relations the most central."

C.S. LEWIS
Preface to *George McDonald: An Anthology*

Thanks, Grandpa. Someday you'll meet all these descendants. And we'll drink a Pepsi and chew a little candy together. And worship. God has blessed us.

You see, right now, you and I are affecting generations to come. One man's life actually marks his children, grandchildren, great-grandchildren, and on and on....

Think about it. By our fathering—good, bad, and ugly—we are actually affecting the leadership of the mid-twenty-second century! What an awesome power!

Start a New Trend

Right about now you may be thinking, "Oh, great! This 'third and fourth generation' thing is so powerful, that I'm doomed." No, you're not. You're not stuck. You're not locked into some prescribed generational pattern. Scripture is full of those who grabbed the high voltage wire of God's transforming power and changed that pattern for His glory. Yes, your heritage will affect you, but it need not spell out your future. You can start a new trend. You may not have come from a healthy family of origin, but you can start one. My Grandpa did. So can you.

So start your own heritage. From this generation forward. Change the course of the river. Change the trends. Change your world. It can be done. Be a man. Stand firm in the faith. Act in love.

Norm Norquist did. Norm is a friend of mine and a fellow elder at Good Shepherd Church—a spiritual patriarch. But his father wasn't. Norm's dad was angrily antagonistic when it came to spiritual things. That created a lot of stress and pain in the home. But Norm determined he would do it differently. He would do it right. He would father a new and healthy family. He would be spiritually oriented. Norm and Dottie had six boys. (Then they "gave up" and adopted two girls.) Today those children have married and had children of their own—lots of children! Because some of them followed their parents' examples and adopted children in addition to their biological children, Norm and Dottie enjoy thirty-one grandchildren, and are still counting. That vibrant Norquist family is at the heart of our church. Grandparents, parents, grandchildren, and now great-grandchildren are following Christ. In just a generation or two, a heritage has been turned completely around spiritually and is on track.

So don't spend a lot of energy fretting about what you didn't get in your family of origin. Don't waste your time casting blame. Blame NEVER helps. Flint McCullugh never spent a day rootin' around where the train had already been. He was too busy envisioning the future. Take that approach. Climb a tree. Dream a future. Draw a plan. Enjoy. Here are a few tips.

A Few Practical Pointers...for Positive Father Power

1. Pursue the Ultimate Father.

This was Grandpa's focus. It was my father's focus. Live for eternity instead of the weekends. Think mission. Think larger than yourself. Give your life away to the Ultimate Father and the people He has sovereignly placed around you. Whether you are married or not, or have children or not, you are a man. You were made to be with other people—a provider, protector, teacher, and friend. Go for it.

2. Model and teach respect for authority.

A father is "a source, a founder, an author." *Author* is the root of *authority*. A father is an authority. He represents the ultimate Author, the ultimate Authority. Teach your children to respect each other, all others, adults in general, and schoolteachers in particular.

3. Help your family see the big picture.

Show your kids how God sees this world. Help them wrestle with eternal perspective. Teach them that life is so much more than holding a job and living at an address. It is mission! Living for the Kingdom. Get involved in a local church—one that takes the Bible, itself, and you seriously.

4. Commit solidly to family unity.

Help everyone understand there will be no isolation or enmity under your roof. Nip it in the bud. Root it out wherever it raises its head. We have a little saying at our house that we repeat regularly, "We will never do it perfectly around here, but we will always do it together." Nothing pleases a father like the oneness of his children. That's true "on earth and in Heaven."

5. Be positive in building family members' confidence.

"You know, honey...you know, son...you are the only you. There'll never be another like you. You have passions, interests, talents, and gifts that make a unique combination. I appreciate you and the way you are. I learn from you."

By consistently building your family's self-esteem, you will ensure that the positive power of fathering (and not the negative) extends across the generations.

And remember, Dad, in the words of an anonymous poet:

I saw tomorrow.
I saw tomorrow marching.
I saw tomorrow marching on little children's feet.
Within their forms and faces her prophecy now complete.
I saw tomorrow look at me from little children's eyes
and thought, how carefully we would teach if we
     were really wise.[1]

Wow! What an opportunity! Make the most of it, Dad. Take hold. Whatever your job or status in life might be, you have no greater—or more powerful—privilege.

A Man Faces Himself

1. Get a paper and pen. Write out a brief plan for carrying out "practical pointers for positive father power." Include one or two specifics for each point, when you plan to do it, and with whom.

2. For each of your children, identify the one trait you possess that you would most like to see develop in that child. Then, with the help of your wife, plan a couple of events or experiences that can assist you in working with that child.

A Man Meets with His Friends

1. Is promise-keeping an important part of your own practice of fathering? Why or why not? How can you improve?

2. In what ways is fatherhood "transgenerational in its power"? Is this a frightening thought to you, or a comforting one? Why?

3. What specific actions are you taking in order to comply with God's orders to you to, "Bring your children up in the discipline and instruction of the Lord"?

4. As they get older, in what ways would you like your sons or daughters to resemble you? Which of your characteristics do you hope they don't mimic?

5. Briefly describe your own family heritage. Has this heritage made it tougher or easier to rear your own family?

6. Comment on the idea that by your fathering, you are affecting the leadership of the mid-twenty-second century.

7. Talk through the five "practical pointers for positive father power" listed on pages 151 and 152. How do you seek to accomplish each one?

Arrows in the Hand of a Warrior:

A Man and His Children, Part 3

Behold, children are a gift of the LORD; the fruit of the womb is a reward.
Like arrows in the hand of a warrior, so are the children of one's youth.
How blessed is the man whose quiver is full of them; they shall not be
ashamed, when they speak with their enemies in the gate
(PSALM 127:3-4).

A S I WRITE these words, I'm looking at three arrows on my desk. They differ from one another. Any archer could see that at a glance. Yet in other ways, they are remarkably similar.

I'm turning one in my hand, now. Feeling the heft and balance of its shaft. Looking down its length to the round edges of its blunt head. It's a target arrow, and a good one. I wouldn't waste my time with anything less. It has plastic vanes instead of feathers—the kind of arrow you'd want for shooting in rainy western Oregon. This second one now...yes, it has a good feel to it, too. A hunting arrow. Smooth shaft. Well balanced. A slightly heavier head, and crafted to a literal razor's edge. It's a "broadhead." Plastic-vaned and intended for wet country hunting. The third one is the kind I carry east of the mountains, over on the dry side. It's basically a twin of the second arrow, but sports neat black and gray feathers instead of plastic.

They're different, these arrows of mine. Each intended for a different impact. Each designed for a different sort of target. They're also very similar; each has been fashioned and crafted, molded and balanced.

They're all intended for flight. They're all intended for a target. They're all intended for maximum impact on that target.

They're good arrows. But then again, they're not much better than the archer who notches them on the bow. They're not much better than the fullness of his draw. They're not much better than the smoothness of his release. No matter how finely crafted those arrows might be, you couldn't pull a guy off the street and expect him to let loose with a seventy-pound bow and nail a target with one of them. Accuracy demands a trained, full draw and a disciplined release.

As I write these words, I'm looking at a picture on my desk.

It's a picture of my three sons—Kent, Blake, and Ryan. They're different, these sons of mine. Unbelievably different. But they're also similar.

Each was crafted by the Lord God in the secret place of his mother's womb. And each was fashioned, balanced, and readied for flight within the four walls of our home.

My three arrows were all designed to leap from the bow and split the air. I enjoy bow hunting, and I intend to *use* these arrows— whether on a cedar bale target or on a bull elk stamping on some back-country ridge on a frosty morning. These arrows aren't for show. They were never intended to stay in a quiver. The quiver is just a vehicle that carries them until they are ready for release. You might say those arrows were *made* to be released. They were made to fly. They were made to pierce a target.

So it is with my sons. They were never intended to stay bunched in the four walls of their childhood home. Yes, the home is a vehicle to fashion and straighten and true and balance those boys. But when the moment comes…young men—and young women—were made to experience flight. Flight to target, flight for maximum impact on that target.

"Like arrows in the hand of a warrior, so are the children of one's youth."

If the arrow misses its mark, is it because it was defective? If the arrow has poor impact, was the arrow weak? Perhaps. But what about the archer who draws the bow? What about his eye for the target, the strength of his draw, the skill of his release?

If, for instance, you only manage a 90 percent draw on your bow, you can lose up to *30 percent* of your impact power. So it's important to relax, apply all of your muscle energy, take a deep breath, and rest at least momentarily at full draw. Then...the release. What a critical moment! No matter how keen your focus, no matter how strong your draw, if you jerk, slip, or fade on the instant of release, the arrow will fly erratically.

Our children were designed by their Creator to make an impact on the world. To live for a reason. To speed toward a goal. To accomplish a purpose. To count for something in God's great scheme of things. Ultimately, of course, they are responsible as individuals before their heavenly Father for the flight they take and the mark they make. Yet parents—and fathers in particular—are also accountable before God. Tender warriors are responsible for releasing those few precious arrows with all the sureness of eye and strength of arm that we can borrow from our God and Father.

Releasing the Arrow

Carol Kuykendall writes:

Letting go is a God-given responsibility as important as love in the parent-child relationship. Without it, without release, children cannot grow. With it, they gain the confidence and independence to seek and reach their potential in life. 'Give your children roots and wings,' the old saying goes. Love them and protect them, nurture them with a strong sense of God and family and then—let them go.[1]

For God's sake, for their sake, for your sake, for the world's sake, for the kingdom's sake, let them go. Give them a full draw, Tender Warriors. Give them a smooth release.

Some time ago, Dr. James Dobson surveyed a group of adult children about their top five concerns as they related to their parents. You might expect that "in-law problems" would have topped that list. Not so. Surprisingly, of the five struggles Dr. Dobson records,[2] that was the *last* on the list. Next to the bottom, in fourth place, was concern over illnesses associated with aging. In third place, these young adults expressed great apprehension over the spiritual welfare of non-Christian parents. The number two heartache was over grandparents who refused the role, who showed little interest in the grandchildren.

The number one issue for these adult children as they sought to relate to their parents—with twice as many expressions of concern as any other difficulty—was the inability or unwillingness of parents to release their grown children.

One woman in the survey wrote: "My mother felt like my leaving home was an insult to her. She couldn't let go. She couldn't realize I needed to become an independent person. She couldn't understand that I no longer needed her physical help, although I still needed her as a person. Quite unintentionally, she retarded my growing up by thirty-five years."

Another lamented, "I'm fifty-four years old, but when I visit my mother, I'm still not allowed to do certain things—such as peel the carrots, even. Because I don't do them correctly. Our relationship is still child/parent. I am still regularly corrected, criticized, and put down."

Any bow hunter will tell you that the release is critical to the accurate flight of the arrow. It's extremely important that your anchor point be consistent. That you think through the release. That the action be fluid. Practiced. Deliberate. Decisive.

If it's not all of these things, you'll have an arrow that flies with a wobbly tail. What you want is an arrow that flies straight and true and balanced. What you want is an arrow that packs a wallop.

So it is with releasing your children.

A surprising number of young parents I counsel seem to have the idea that everything will somehow just "come naturally" at those critical stages of raising a family. Somehow, they reason, when the skills and wisdom are needed, they'll just *be* there, like ripe apples ready to be plucked. Nice thought, but life as I've seen it doesn't work that way. Skillful parenting does *not* come naturally. Wisdom and balance do *not* come naturally. This is especially true in a culture such as ours, so utterly confused, so wildly off-course, so pitiful in its attempts to sail turbulent seas with neither keel nor rudder. It's vital that we think carefully and rationally and biblically *in advance* about family matters... and releasing children is one of the most critical issues of all.

Letting Go Is Not Easy

Why is it so hard to let go? Why is it so difficult to draw the bow and let fly? Because it contradicts everything we are as parents! We *fear* our loss of influence. We *dread* our declining parental control. And in our human nature, it's natural for any of us to attempt to manipulate others to get our own way. That's particularly true with those who have become so dear to us, those who have hatched in our own little nest. After all, we have been responsible *from birth* for their provision and protection. We have shielded them. We have prayed for them. We have agonized over them. We have fought for them. We have sought to defend them through virtually every circumstance. And, let's face it, this business of "letting go" diminishes our role. That never feels good to a human being.

But let go we must! At a turning point in his ministry, John the Baptist said of the Lord Jesus, "He must increase, I must decrease." That's the role of the parent with our own little home-grown disciples. They must increase; but we must decrease. Their personal responsibility to the Lord must increase; their personal responsibility to Dad and Mom must decrease.

Dr. Dobson writes:

We want to rise like a mighty shield to protect them from life's sting. To hold them snugly within the safety of our embrace. Yet there are times when we must let them struggle. Children can't grow without taking risks. Toddlers can't walk initially without falling down. Students cannot learn without facing some hardships. And ultimately, an adolescent cannot enter young adulthood until we release him from our protective custody.[3]

Letting go takes an act of the will because it contradicts so much of what we are, and because it involves significant pain. There is very little on this earth so strong as the love of a parent for a child. When you have bonded over a lifetime that began with utter dependence on you and has developed with progressive independence from you, it's very, very difficult to relax the white knuckles of that parental grip. There is a sense of loss, there is a sense of disorientation.

Erma Bombeck, in classic Bombeckian style, made these remarks as her last child marched off to school:

My excuse for everything just got on that bus. My excuse for not dieting, not getting a full time job, not cleaning house, not reupholstering the furniture, not going back to school, not having order in my life, not cleaning the oven. It is the end of an era. Now what do I do for the next twenty years of my life?[24]

That's another reason it's hard to let go. It's not only painful, it's also *confusing*. You would think that smothering your child and abandoning your child would be on opposite ends of the spectrum. But for most parents, they're a razor's edge apart. *When am I smothering? When am I abandoning? When am I doing and saying too much? When am I doing and saying too little? When am I interfering? When am I neglecting?*

It's not easy to know! There doesn't seem to be any in-between. Am I building my child's confidence, or am I actually bruising that confidence? That's why releasing must be thought through so carefully over the years. It's a process that cries out for multiple counselors, the closest of partnerships with your mate, and the boundless wisdom of God Himself.

But, difficult as that act of will may be, there are also some real positive sides to it. There is a sense of accomplishment. There is a sense of completion. There is a sense of rightness. It is *done*. As Jesus said, "I've done what the Father asked Me to do." Despite the pang of loss, there is a deep, underlying sense of relief when the release actually takes place.

Letting Go Is a Process

Letting go, however is a process, not an act. It's a lifelong mind-set, not an impulsive decision. Whether you speak of bow hunting or parenting, a smooth release demands constant practice. You have to do it over and over again, or you'll never master it.

Launching your sons and daughters is an act of the will that is *progressive* in nature. The goal is to release a child to adulthood and full responsibility for his or her own well-being under God, according to His purposes. An act of the will is a decision. It's a thought process. It's deliberate and intelligent. It's not something that "just comes naturally," but rather requires intelligent, skillful discipline to accomplish.

So our God, in His magnificent wisdom, provides us multiple opportunities to practice the releasing of our children before that climactic release when they sever ties and leave home for good. He allows us poignant and memorable checkpoints along the way. If you stop and think about it, parents must begin releasing at the moment of birth. There is that small matter of cutting the umbilical cord. SNIP! From the sacred moment of conception, there had been an intricate, intimate sharing of two life systems. And then...SNIP! That sharing is over. Suddenly you're cradling a little *independent* life system. A lovely little human being.

There are many, many more such SNIPS over the years, aren't there?

Following birth, there's the weaning of the child from the breast or bottle. The graduation to strained squash and other such appetizing fare. It's one of many practiced releases.

Do you remember the first baby-sitter? What an act of releasing that is! I've tried to blot that particular memory from my mind, but it refuses to disappear. Suffice it to say, it doesn't go all that smoothly for parent or child sometimes. Do you recall the first time you left your children at home *without* a baby-sitter? I'll never forget that particular release attempt. We had rehearsed all the do's and don'ts with our boys so carefully. *As soon as the sun goes down, you're inside. You lock the door, you stay there. Anybody comes to the door, it's too bad. You don't open the door. You don't know anybody. You don't recognize anybody. You just stay there. We'll be gone for one hour and then we'll be back.*

The hour came and went, darkness arrived, and we turned down our street toward home. And behold! There in our headlights, spaced evenly across the road, were three little boys. Waiting for their parents. Little goofballs! That precipitated a warm discussion behind closed doors. But it was part of the release point. And even the best of arrows gets a wobbly send-off sometimes. (That's what "practiced releases" are all about.)

Do you remember the first day of kindergarten? How about that first bicycle? You have to stand back a little bit, don't you? And there have to be some crashes if some skill is going to be developed. Thomas Huxley, the English biologist, wrote, "There is great practical benefit in making a few failures early in life." Bicycles have a way of bringing them.

On the august occasion of our middle son's graduation from kindergarten, I remember one rather traumatic release point. It was going to be a big evening for little Blake. Cap and gown. Pomp and circumstance. A solemn launch into the mysterious realms of elementary school. That afternoon, our little graduate was cruising on his bike out in front of the house. Contemplating his advanced age, perhaps, he was riding with no hands on the handlebars. For some reason, he turned his head for a moment to look over at the house. That's when he encountered the parked car. We rushed him to the emergency room and winced as the doctor cut a swath of hair right down the middle of his head in order to stitch him up. As a result, he was the only kid at kindergarten graduation sporting a reverse mohawk.

Do you remember your child's first stay overnight at a friend's house? That's a practiced release. How about the day he or she obtained a learner's permit for driving? Horrors! Walking through the glass doors of the Department of Motor Vehicles for that all-important exam, your son or daughter steps into a first experience with civil authority.

Do you remember when he or she got that coveted driver's license and drove off down the road for the first time? One such experience is etched so vividly in Linda's memory that the words spoken that day have become a proverb and a byword at the Weber household. They are now the normal and customary words we share with one another virtually every time we part. As Blake was about to drive off, he somehow anticipated his mother's thoughts. "Bye Mom," he called out with a wry grin. *"Hope to see you again!"*

It was yet another practiced release. If you've been through it, you can perhaps remember praying for some kind of shockingly traumatic but nonexpensive incident to impress your teen with the incredible destructive power of those four-wheeled missiles.

Remember the first summer job? Your child was suddenly responsible to *someone else* to do good, solid, consistent work.

Do you remember the first time your teen walked through the front door with a member of the opposite sex?

Do you remember college? The first time away from home for an extended season?

There are a thousand practiced releases. Each can help us develop our technique; each can bring us to that strong draw and smooth release of a disciplined archer.

Let your children experience life as they grow up in your home. Let them experience consistent and appropriate release. As David wrote, "Then our sons in their youth will be like well-nurtured plants, and our daughters will be like pillars carved to adorn a palace" (Psalm 144:12, NIV). Or as Jeremiah noted, "It is good for a man that he should bear the yoke in his youth" (Lamentations 3:27).

So start practicing now with that target in mind. From the moment of birth to the majesty of maturity, practice release.

Nancy McConnell observes, "Being a mother is a lot like teaching a child to ride a bicycle. You have to know when to hold on and when to let go. If you lack this courage to let go, you're going to get very tired of running along beside."[5] There's a world of wisdom in that observation for mothers *and* fathers.

It's important that the arrow know when it's being released. It ought to register in that arrow's pointy broadhead: *This is a special moment. This is a special privilege. This is a departure from the norm. Dad or Mom is letting go a little right now.*

What's the Target?

What then, are we releasing our children to? What's the target?

First of all, you are releasing them to adulthood. You're letting them grow up. You are releasing your son to manhood and your daughter to womanhood. If you're diligent in searching God's Word, you will have a clear view of what the "bull's-eye" for manhood and womanhood look like. You will understand what a man and woman were made for. You will release your sons to become tender warriors, provisionaries, and men who stay and stay and stay. You will release your daughters to be what God fashioned a woman to be: strong in companionship ability, and off the charts in nurturing skills and the development of other human beings. A helpmate suitable.

How can you hope to aim those arrows of yours without a vision of the target? Life is too short to make random shots into the air. Time doesn't allow for a slipshod "I shot an arrow into the air; it fell to earth I know not where" kind of thinking. Those God-given arrows of yours are too precious to waste.

In the majority of cases, the "target" for your boys and girls will include preparation for marriage. God designed us as men and women, and He designed us for marriage. Not that it's impossible to be a fulfilled and completed person apart from matrimony, but it's normal for a human being to look forward to a permanent marital union. God created us to live out specific roles within that marriage relationship. A man's role is not a woman's role, and a woman's role is not a man's role. As we study God's intentions for those roles and live them out in our marriages before the watching eyes of our children, we prepare them for their own marriages and homes.

Our goal, says one insightful writer, is "to produce kids who can emotionally leave home, kids who can come to love somebody else more than they love their parents."[6] That's a wise and mature statement. We release them to their manhood, we release them to their womanhood, and then we release them to full responsibility for their own well-being. That includes responsibility

—for their own living place
—for their own bills
—for their own health
—for their own insurance
—for their own relationships
—for their own walk with God

and for all the other things that are part of life and well-being on this planet. Release them to full responsibility for those necessary burdens.

In his own inimitable way, Bill Cosby described this phenomenon in a commencement address at the University of South Carolina.

All across this great nation people are graduating and hearing they are going forth. My concern is whether they know where forth is. The road home is already paved. Forth is not back home. We love you and we are proud of you, and we are not tired of you…but we could *get* tired of you. Forth could be next door to us, but you pay the rent.[7]

No Strings Attached

Once those arrows are launched, by the way, they leave the string. That means no strings attached. There should be a complete freedom from rule. That arrow is flying on its own now. That means there will be no more demands from home. No more directives. No more orders. No more discipline. Neither should there be any more heroic parental rescue missions! Dialing "9-1-1" ought not to ring automatically on Mom and Dad's bedroom phone.

A loyal love, the kind of loyal love demonstrated in scripture, does not remove consequences from decisions or choices—however ill-advised. That thought may be a little frightening to the recent initiate into the adult world. But with that tinge of fear comes an exhilarating sense of responsibility, a strong sense of encouragement and affirmation. *My parents have loved me. My parents have encouraged me. My parents are cheering me on. My parents have not abandoned me. My parents are not glad to be rid of me, but affirm me in my launching and the direction I'm taking. They have completed their task. I have roots—and now I have wings.* A grown child ought to know these things. It's the sort of inner assurance that brings a clear sense of controlling their own destiny under God.

This momentous final release is just one more family milestone that has been muddled and muddied by our contemporary culture. That release should be obvious, pronounced, deliberate, and clearly recognized by the participants.

There should be some recognizable rite of passage.

I'll never forget the wedding of one of my best college friends, John Engstrom, years ago. Actually it wasn't the wedding itself that impressed me as much as something that happened at the rehearsal dinner. Mrs. Engstrom, John's mom, was seated at the front table with John, his bride, and the bride's parents. At a particular time at the dinner, Mrs. Engstrom stood up and pulled out a beautifully wrapped box. She unwrapped it, and with great ceremony, displayed one of her favorite old aprons. Holding the apron high for everyone to see, she reached into her purse and brought out a big pair of scissors. With a flourish, she snipped off the apron strings and handed them to John's bride-to-be.

"Never again," she said, "will I have the same place in John Engstrom's life. You are now the woman in his life."

It was a moment of formal releasing, in front of many witnesses. And the most significant witnesses of all were a young bride and groom. It was a profound moment…but a joyful one, too. There was a feeling of rightness (and rite-ness) about it all.

Men's movement writers Robert Bly, Sam Keen, Robert Moore, and others are right in pointing out that this "coming of age" ceremony is a huge missing element in American manhood. There is no sense of launching. There is no sense of release. There is no proud, climactic moment. There is no rite of passage into manhood. All the tribal cultures have experienced it in the past. The knights of old experienced it. A military officer experiences it. The moment of release. The moment of commission.

One of the things we need to restore is a sense of release, a moment in time when everybody involved in our child's life realizes, "This young person is now responsible for his or her own life." That can come in any number of ways. With my own parents, it wasn't a formal event at all. It was a moment none of us would have or could have rehearsed. I don't know how deliberate or practiced it was, but I do remember it as vividly now as the day it happened. It took place at a train depot. I was off for college. For the first time in my life I was leaving home for an extended season. *I saw it in their eyes.* It was strong. It was an unforgettable moment. In later years, my mother would say that from that moment on, it was never the same. It was more than getting on a train for Illinois. It was leaving childhood.

We haven't married off any of our children, but we released one of them last spring. It was one of those increasingly rare opportunities when all five of us were together. We were in Lexington, Massachusetts, just off of the Lexington Green, where the little arch reads, "The Birthplace of Freedom." It seemed to be an appropriate place to meet and release our firstborn son to his own authority and his own life. It was not far from where "the shot heard 'round the world" was fired. There we decided to "fire" one of our own, praying it might have significant impact. Linda and I had written a message on a parchment, and then framed it. It was a document that noted his graduation from our family. In our minds, it was a more valuable and potent document than the sheepskin he had received from his college. Here is what Kent read that evening on the Lexington Green.

"As arrows in the hand of a warrior, so are the children of one's youth. How blessed is the man whose quiver is full of them."

To a world very much needing his character, his gifts, his skill, and his love for Christ, we, Stu and Linda Weber, do proudly and humbly announce in the manner of our heavenly Father, this is our beloved son, Kent Byron Weber, in whom we are well pleased. Like an arrow fashioned not to remain in the quiver, but to be released into the heart of its target, we release Kent to adulthood. We know him to be thoughtful, capable, and mature. He is the message we release to a world we will never see. He is a man. We release him to his manhood and all of its responsibilities. To the finding and cherishing of a godly and supportive wife, to the begetting and raising by God's grace and design of believing children. And to the commission of the Lord Jesus Christ Himself to go into all the world, making followers of all people, teaching them to observe the rich and life-giving truths of His holy scriptures.

Kent, we love you, we're extremely proud of you, and we release you to the target of being all you can be in Christ. You will always be our son. You will never again be our little boy. Thank you, Kent, for having graced our lives with your remarkable sonship. You have blessed us richly.

"Be strong, therefore, and show yourself a man" (1 Kings 2:2).

"Be on the alert, stand firm in the faith, act like men, be strong. Let all that you do be done in love" (1 Corinthians 16:13).

Your very fulfilled parents,

Stu and Linda Weber,
Mom and Dad, Spring 1992

For Kent, there was a moment in time when he stepped over the border into manhood. We were with him in that moment and had the privilege to witness it. Kent's younger brothers were there, too, watching, pondering, waiting for their own moments of release. There is no doubt in Kent's mind that he is an adult, and that he is charged with responsibility before God for his own life.

Millennia ago, the invention of the bow and arrow changed the face of warfare forever. For the first time, a warrior could impact a battle scene from a great distance. Similarly, our children are the only messages we'll send to a world we'll never see. They are the only provision we have for impacting a world at a distance.

May God grant us the strength to draw our bows to the full and the wisdom to release our arrows with practiced skill.

As time draws to a close on this darkened planet, surely every arrow must count.

A Man Faces Himself

1. Develop, on paper, an appropriate "rite of passage" for each of your children. Discuss with your wife how the two of you can actually plan for and produce this important event.

2. Develop for each of your children a picture of their own future. Concentrate on life essentials not career or vocation. To help you in this most critical project, consider attending a Family Life Parenting Conference in your region. (Call 501-223-8663 for information.) Plan how you can communicate this picture to each child—through both verbal encouragement and meaningful actions. Make sure you have a clear picture of the "target" you have in mind. Then communicate it well.

A Man Meets with His Friends

1. In what ways are children like arrows? Meditate on this analogy. How can drawing it out make you a more effective father?

2. Will it be easy or hard for you to release your children when it comes time to do so? Why?

3. At what stage are you in the progressive "release" of your children? In what smaller ways have you already "released" them? What did you learn from each of these releases? What did they learn from each?

4. Describe the target you are developing toward which you hope to release your children. Be as specific as you can be.

5. When your parents released you, did you know it? Were there strings attached? If so, what was the result? If not, do you know anyone who labors under such a situation? Describe what you see.

6. Brainstorm for a bit on appropriate "rites of passage" for your children as they enter adulthood.

7. Imagine some possible futures for your children. Without referring to a specific career, what would you like to see them accomplish in their lifetimes? Do they understand your hopes for them?

Real Men Stand Together:

A Man and His Friends, Part 1

I had no rest for my spirit,
not finding Titus my brother…
(2 CORINTHIANS 2:13).

*Y*OUR LOVE TO ME *was more wonderful than the love of* *women.*" What words are these? Perverted words? Twisted words? The words of some pathetic sexual deviate?

No. A war-hardened veteran penned these words after his best buddy fell in battle. They were written by a warrior, with the piercing grief only a soldier mourning for a comrade-in-arms could begin to understand.

Twisted words? No. They are words straight and true—a swift, clean arrow shot from the heart of Scripture. David wrote these words after the death of his friend Jonathan on the bloody slopes of Mount Gilboa. What the son of Jesse expressed without shame in that lament was something that has burned deep in the soul of every man in one way or another for generations beyond memory.

A desire for friendship man to man. A desire for friendship with nothing between. A yearning for friendship so real, so strong, so compelling, it is willing to share everything about itself and make deep and powerful promises.

Down deep at the core, every man needs a man friend.

Down deep at the core, every man needs a brother to lock arms with.

Down deep at the core, every man needs a soul mate.

Men Need Friends Who Are Men

Yes, beyond question, our wives are to be our most intimate companions. We're to be willing to die for our wives and our children instantly, and many of us are ready to do just that. But within the willingness to die for family and home, something inside us longs for someone to die *with*...someone to die *beside*...someone to lock step with. Another man with a heart like our own.

That's what David was saying about Prince Jonathan. Every warrior needs a fellow soldier. Every fighter pilot needs a wing man. David was demonstrating something that even the U.S. Army, in all its relational ineptitude, understands. When you're going to do something that stretches the very fabric of your soul, like get through nine weeks of army Ranger school at Fort Benning, Georgia, you're going to need a buddy. A "Ranger Buddy." Those two words mean a world to me. It was my Ranger Buddy, Lou Francis, who clung to my arm and I to his through sixty-three days of unbelievable physical and mental trauma. Together, we made it through the toughest experience either of us had ever faced to that point in our lives.

Some might argue with me, but I know of no more intense training regimen in the U.S. military. These guys know how to take a young man and stretch him tendon by tendon—physical tendon by physical tendon, emotional tendon by emotional tendon.

I remember well that last, most intense phase of our training, called "Unconventional Warfare." We were in the swamps of western Florida in the dead of winter. I would never have dreamed Florida could be so cold. We were at the end of a several-day patrol, and nearly at the end of ourselves. We'd been without sleep for most of those days, and very nearly without food. Our particular mission required us to proceed to a certain set of coordinates at the corner of our map. Unfortunately, those coordinates happened to be on the other side of the Yellow River.

We had been staggering knee-deep through the numbing water of a cypress swamp for what seemed like eons. The temperature was below freezing, and our bodies were at the ragged edge of our endurance. The "knees" of the cypress trees, invisible under the black waters, savaged our shins and ankles. And the river was still somewhere ahead of us.

When we finally reached the river, it was practically indistinguishable from the water we'd been wading in. The only way we could tell it was a river was by the rapidly moving current and the lack of cypress trees.

Our goal was a piece of higher ground on the other side. We knew we couldn't get our clothes wet or the cold would finish us. So we stripped down to our skimpy briefs and, as we'd been trained, made a little float out of our two ponchos, with our rifles and packs protected. Wading out into the icy water, we were surprised by the strength of the current. Though we were both fair swimmers, we found ourselves being swept further and further downstream. It was fearsome. Reaching back for a burst of strength from some final untapped reserve, both of us began kicking with all our might. The effort was rewarded as we inched toward the slimy bank and finally achieved it.

We crawled out of the water, blue from the cold, trailing bits of river weed and slime. So delighted to be alive. So exultant at having reached our goal. I remember our looking into each other's eyes and then spontaneously throwing our arms around each other. We stood there for a moment on the bleak winter bank of the Yellow River, two dripping, shivering young men in their briefs, laughing and crying and holding on to each other as if we'd never let go.

If we each live to be a hundred, I expect neither of us will ever forget the camaraderie of that moment.

We'd made it. We'd stayed alive. The two of us.

Every man, whether he admits it or not, needs a Ranger Buddy. Every man needs someone with whom he can face adversity and death. Emerson wrote: "We take care of our health. We lay up money. We make our roof tight. We make our clothing sufficient. But who provides wisely that he shall not be wanting in the best property of all, friends—friends strong and true?"

Why Men Don't Have Friends Who Are Men

A professor at Southern Methodist University had this to say after ten years of study on the subject:

> To say that men have no intimate friends seems on the surface too harsh, and it raises quick objections from most men. But the data indicates that it is not far from the truth. Even the most intimate of friendships (of which there are few) rarely approach the depth of disclosure a woman commonly has with other women.... men, who neither bare themselves nor bear one another, are buddies in name only.[1]

Oh, we may *want* that friendship. Every man, whether he admits it or not, walks around with a hollow place in his chest, wondering if he is the only one. But there is something within us that keeps us at arm's length. *What is that something that keeps men distant and friendless?*

I saw a man about my age the other day in a crowded parking lot. If one Vietnam vet can spot another, then I knew this man for what he was and what he had endured. I felt an immediate love for him. He was on crutches, and one pant leg was folded and pinned up to the top. Everyone in that busy lot seemed to avert their eyes from this disabled gentleman. It's something we find ourselves doing in that sort of situation, isn't it? One glance tells us something isn't normal. Something isn't right. Something's missing. In the physical sense, this man wasn't "all there."

I think most of us would have to admit that when it comes to open and vulnerable man-to-man friendships, we are walking on one leg. We're really not "all there." Something's missing. Something's pinned up and empty in our souls. We may be "kings" and "warriors," but we seem to have lost something of the tender side. So we're really one-legged men. We simply don't know how to fellowship.

If the most basic definition of "fellowship" is two fellows in one ship, then we don't know what to do with ourselves when we're out at sea. In a fine fresh wind on a starry night when we stand together at the bow looking out into the dark, mysterious depths—on a night that cries out for deep talk and sharing of the soul—we lapse into silence or mutter idly about how many chunks of salt pork it takes to fill a barrel below decks.

Kent Hughes, a thoughtful pastor in the Midwest, makes this observation about our culture:

There has been an interesting development in suburban architecture. Long gone are the days when homes all had large front porches, with easy access to the front door enabling one to become quickly acquainted with others in the neighborhood.

In the 1990s we have architecture which speaks more directly to our current values. The most prominent part of the house seems to be the two-or three-car garage. Inside are huge bathrooms with skylights and walk-in closets larger than the bedroom I grew up in. Modern architecture employs small living and dining rooms and now smaller kitchens as well, because entertaining is no longer a priority. Today's homes boast smaller yards and an increasing incidence of high fences.

The old adage that "a man's house is his castle" is actually coming true today. His castle's moat is his front lawn, the drawbridge his driveway, and the portcullis his automatic garage door through which he passes with electronic heraldry. Once inside, he removes his armor and attends to house and hearth until daybreak, when he assumes his executive armament and, briefcase in hand, mounts his steed—perhaps a Bronco or a Mustang—presses the button, and rides off to the wars. Today's homes reflect our modern values of individualism, isolation and privatization."[2]

Individualism...isolation...privatization. These are destructive words. Painful words. They have an empty sound to them, don't they? They leave a hollowness in our chest.

Patrick Morley, author of *The Man in the Mirror,* wryly observes that while most men could recruit six pallbearers, "hardly anyone has a friend he can call at 2:00 A.M."[3]

Referring to a recent study in Britain, sociologist Marion Crawford stated: Middle-aged men and women had considerably different definitions of friendship. By an overwhelming margin, women talked about "trust and confidentiality," while men described a friend as "someone I could go out with" or "someone whose company I enjoy." For the most part men's friendships revolve around activities, while women's revolve around sharing.[4]

We're not talking now about a golfing buddy. We're talking about somebody we can be soulish with.

Why are these things true? I have my theories. If we men are comprised of steel and velvet, most of us feel more comfortable with the steel. We find it easier to live out the "provide and protect" functions than the "mentor and friend" functions. It stands to reason that the hard side dominates the tender side. Many of us have underdeveloped tender sides because we've been taught wrongly about manhood. Not deliberately, but wrongly. We need to become more tender. The warrior in us wants to be strong and needs to be strong. But we don't want to admit to any chinks in our armor. We don't want to admit to any vulnerabilities—*the very element that is essential for true friendships.* Oh, the vulnerabilities are *there,* all right. But most of us have learned to carefully hide them. Some might call that "manliness." Others might more accurately label it for what it is: *dishonesty.*

Friendship requires honesty. Friendship requires trust. So it also—no way around it—requires vulnerability. I think that's the bottom line of this no-friends syndrome in us men. And it's spelled P-R-I-D-E.

We all want to think of ourselves as some kind of warrior, as some kind of man's man. Unfortunately though, as much as we love John Wayne, there is a side to the Duke that never emerged. All you ever saw was the steel. You never saw the velvet unless it was for a fleeting moment in *She Wore a Yellow Ribbon.* John Wayne left us with the impression that real men stand alone. And so they do…when it is necessary. But the only reason it seems "necessary" most of the time is our stubborn, unyielding pride.

Real men stand together. We need to start thinking that way. Real men need one another. Real soldiers love each other.

Hal Moore and Joe Galloway capture that love powerfully in the prologue to their great book about the Vietnam War, *We Were Soldiers Once…and Young:*

Another war story, you say? Not exactly, for on the more important levels this is a love story, told in our own words and by our own actions. We were the children of the 1950s and we went where we were sent because we loved our country....

We went to war because our country asked us to go, because our new president, Lyndon B. Johnson, ordered us to go, but more importantly because we saw it as our duty to go. That is one kind of love.

Another and far more transcendent love came to us unbidden on the battlefields, as it does on every battlefield in every war man has ever fought. We discovered in that depressing, hellish place, where death was our constant companion, that we loved each other. We killed for each other, we died for each other, and we wept for each other. And in time we came to love each other as brothers. In battle our world shrank to the man on our left and the man on our right and the enemy all around. We held each other's lives in our hands and we learned to share our fears, our hopes, our dreams as readily as we shared what little else good came our way.[5]

It's always been that way. Real soldiers stand together. It was that way in Hal Moore's Ia Drang Valley in 1965, and it was that way long before in the hot sands of Alexander's ancient Near East. Real world conquerors stand arm in arm. Alexander the Great was "great," I suppose, because at one time he owned most of the habitable real estate on the planet. His secret weapon was something called the "Macedonian Phalanx," which was little more than a simple military formation with a straightforward mandate: *You never go into battle without the man beside you.*

The Macedonian Phalanx was a formation that allowed the man's weak flank to be protected by his buddy. With his shield in his left hand and his sword in the right, a soldier thrusting with his blade could find his right side exposed, vulnerable to the enemy's spear or sword. In the Macedonian formation, the warrior had a trusted man guarding the area where he was most exposed. Although Alexander came along centuries after David, I think the son of Jesse would have called such a companion, "the man of my right hand." Where I am most vulnerable and exposed, that's where I want the man of my right hand.

Dr. Charles Sell writes: "Men who have neglected intimate friendships with other men have far greater difficulty handling the midlife turmoil. These men are also devastated at retirement because their whole basis of significance and identity evaporates, and they're left without a network of friends or support."[6]

Close friendship with a man or a woman is rarely experienced by the American male. Author David Smith asserts: "Men find it hard to accept that they need the fellowship of other men. The simple request, 'Let's have lunch together' is likely to be followed with the response, 'Sure, what's up?'"[7]

Can you imagine women saying that to each other? My wife calls your wife and says, "Let's have lunch." Your wife says, "Great, here's my calendar. Where shall we go?" But a man will say, by implication, "What's going on? What's your problem? Why are you doing this?"

Dr. Smith continues: "The message is clear: The independent man doesn't feel he needs the company of another man. In fact, the image of the independent man is that he has few if any emotional needs. Therefore, men must manufacture nonemotional reasons for being together..."[8]

Most of us think we have to conjure up "practical"reasons or excuses for picking up the phone and calling another man. That's part of the myth that says I have few, if any, emotional needs. If men get together, it's because, in Dr. Smith's words:

A business deal must be discussed or a game must be played. Men often use drinking as an excuse to gather together. Rarely do men plan a meeting together simply because they have a need to enjoy each other's company.

Even when men are frequently together, their social interaction begins and remains at a superficial level. Just how long can conversations about politics and sports be nourishing to the human spirit? The same male employees can have lunch together for years and years and still limit their conversations to sports, politics, and dirty jokes, and comments about the sexual attractiveness of selected female workers in their office or plant.[9]

A Willingness to Go Deeper

Going beyond those surface subjects requires transparency. What transparency says at the bottom of it all is, "I really need you. I'm going to take the risk and be honest enough to tell you who I am."

Someone pointed out a moving little piece from a magazine to me. Because it deals with relationships, I think we Tender Warriors can learn something from it.

The woman who wrote the article states:

One day the doorbell rang and there stood my beloved brother. It was a delightful surprise. His work as an executive of an international petroleum company keeps him out of the country most of the time, so his visits are rare, unexpected and usually really brief.

It seemed as if he'd just arrived when after an hour, he got up to say good-bye. I felt tears sliding down my cheeks. He asked why I was crying. Hesitating, I said, "Because I simply don't want you to go." He gave me a surprised look. He went to the phone and left a message for the pilot of his company's plane.

We had a wonderful forty-eight hours together. But I suffered a nagging feeling that my selfishness had caused him great inconvenience. Because I had told him I needed him.

Some time later my brother received an important award for his contributions to the oil industry. A reporter asked him at the time, "Is this the greatest honor that you've received?"

"No," he said, "my sister gave me my greatest honor the day she cried because she didn't want me to leave. That's the only time in my life anyone ever cried because they didn't want me to leave. It was then that I discovered the most precious gift one human being can ever bestow on another is to let him know he is really needed."[10]

That's transparency. That's the destination toward which we must journey. Yes, sometimes our childhood patterns keep us from progressing on that journey. If children are to be seen and not heard, if boys don't cry, then we tend not to be very candid about our hurts and needs.

A Determination to Practice

Practice, practice, practice sharing your emotions. Find some moment in your week that's been especially emotional for you, and then pick out that friend whose name is turning over in your mind and heart today, and go share your emotions with that friend. Start at whatever level. If you need to prime the pump, start with your wife. Most women would treasure a husband's attempt to climb out of his shell.

I remember when I began trying—really trying—to express some honest emotion to my wife. It was like learning to speak all over again. It took some stuttering and stammering, but I had a growing desire to let her know what was going on inside me. I recall one night in particular. It was a number of years ago, following our middle son's high school basketball awards program.

Blake followed his older brother Kent at Barlow High School. Kent was big and tall and mobile and made a name for himself as a starter on the varsity squad. Blake was smaller and shorter. He didn't have the obvious physical advantages of his brother. It was a little intimidating to think of finding a niche at a high school where guards were a dime a dozen.

But he did make the team. Before the season began, the coach said, "I wish we could start twelve guys. Hey, we'd kill everybody in the league! But the rules say we have to start five. So I want you to know that we're going to start five, and then we're going to have three or four substitutes, role players as we call them. Beyond that, we're going to have three or four practice players. Whether you believe me or not, guys, the starters and the role players and the practice players are all essential to this team."

Blake chose to believe the coach. He ended up being one of the practice players, but he stuck with the program. He practiced hard and stayed ready. Still, he didn't get into the games too much unless they were substantially ahead or substantially behind. So in the course of the season he played a limited number of minutes.

When the awards ceremony came, Linda and I sat together in the high school cafeteria, listening to Coach Johnson announce the awards. Every year, the two most coveted awards were the Most Valuable Player trophy and the Most Inspirational Player trophy. Coach went into the usual long buildup prior to the "inspirational" award, talking about what a certain young man had meant to the team and to his teammates. Finally, he called out the name…"Blake Weber." He may not have had as much playing time, but he spent his energy encouraging others. He had marked his team.

Something happened inside of me that night. I experienced more sensations than I could readily describe. My heart filled with potent waves of emotion. This was the boy I had been so concerned about because he had to walk in the big shoes of his brother. This was my middle guy, surrounded by two brothers with individualistic personalities. This was the kid who, in years past, I was most afraid would struggle with positive self-image. And even though he got into the game sparingly, even though he barely got a chance to really handle the ball, he had such a positive self-image he won the Most Inspirational Player award. I tingled all over.

I remember driving home with Linda that night, opening and closing my mouth a few times before I could get out any words. It wasn't easy for me to talk about something so personally moving, something so deep inside. The old Stu Weber would have kept it bottled and corked on a dusty back shelf of memory. But that night I didn't want to put those feelings in a bottle. I didn't want them gathering dust on a back shelf. So I took the plunge. Staring straight ahead at the road, I finally said, "Lindy, I just want to tell you what's happening inside of me—what happened when his name was called tonight." Bit by bit—and then in a great rush—the pride and gratitude and wonder of it all came out through my lips. *And it felt so good.*

Practice sharing your emotions. Find somebody who seems more relaxed and skilled at it, and watch how they do it. When you open your Bible, spend some time in the psalms with David. This was a true man's man and mighty warrior who knew how to put his emotions into words. He knew how to spill his guts before God. He knew how to cry out his fears and discouragement and hopes and joys. You can see the whole range of feeling in this man's words. Joyful laughter. Shouts of praise. Burning anger. The deep hurt of betrayal. Paralyzing fear. Overwhelming waves of discouragement. Sweet relief. Overflowing gratitude. Love. It's all there. He's all over the emotional, spiritual map. His journey is the spiritual journey of a Tender Warrior, recorded forever in Scripture for warriors like you and me who want to follow in his wake.

Practice with your wife. Practice with the psalms of David before your God. And practice with other men, too.

I have one friend in particular who knows me—my marriage, my heart, my life. And I know him and his. As I'm out driving around on my errands during the course of a week, I often find myself thinking about him, praying for him. (Now when I'm out on my hospital calls or other business and think of my wife, I try to stop and give her a phone call. That was a *gargantuan* step for me to take as I've been struggling to learn to speak her language. It has taken a lot for me to remember to stop, dial her number, and say, "Hey, I was just thinking of you." She always appreciates that.)

I decided to take another massive step. I decided to try that with my friend. I was in Chicago. At O'Hare airport. There were thirty minutes between flights, and I picked up a telephone and called him.

I almost found myself wishing he wouldn't be home. I almost choked and hung up when I heard his voice on the other end. *What in the world am I doing? What in the world is he going to think?* But I didn't choke. I heard myself saying into the mouthpiece, "I have no reason for calling you except to say I've had you in my mind today. I've had you in my heart." That was not easy for me to do. But just a few minutes later, I was on that next flight to who knows where and I was glad I had done it. We had a good conversation. I was encouraged.

Small Steps Pay Off

When my father was in World War II, he made friends with a young man named Joe Carter. They were young draftees, plucked out of a peaceful civilian life and thrown into the same barracks at training camp. For a good chunk of the war, they were together. Serving together. Sweating together. Dreaming together of home. It has been over fifty years since they last saw each other. But every year, without fail, my dad gets a birthday card from Joe Carter in the mail.

It's hard to believe that friendship started when my dad walked across the barracks one afternoon to offer a guy named Joe one of the chocolate chip cookies he'd just received in a package from home. Dad is now in his seventies. And every once in awhile, he will pause and look out the window with a distant stare. Then, with a smile on the corner of his lips, he'll say, "You know…I should grab a train and go see my friend, Joe."

A fifty-year friendship sprang from a single chocolate chip cookie. It's that way sometimes. All it takes is breaking the ice. All it takes is walking across the barracks. Or across the hall. Or across the street. Or across the room to pick up the phone. It takes a willingness to choke back some pride and reach out a hand.

Are you giving yourself to anyone? Are you opening up to anyone? Do any of your fellow soldiers know where the chinks in your armor might be? Are you looking for a soul mate, a Ranger Buddy?

Some dark day when your knees are weak, the current is swift, and the water is cold, you will be glad you did.

A Man Faces Himself

1. Ready? Swallow. Pick up the phone. Call your best friend just to see how he's doing—no other agenda! Tell him that's why you're calling.

2. If you're not used to sharing your emotions, pick a time and a place with your best friend where you can practice. Talk about moving moments, events, or incidents in your past. Gradually work to those in the present.

A Man Meets with His Friends

1. How do you react to King David's words about his friend Jonathan: "Your love to me was more wonderful than the love of women"? What elements of true and wholesome friendship do you think David has in mind?

2. How would you describe your own friendships with other men? Casual? Close? Intimate? Non-existent? How might you improve them?

3. Do you have someone you consider your "Ranger Buddy"? If so, describe your relationship. If not, how might you work to obtain such a friend?

4. Evaluate the statement: "Real men stand together. Real men need one another. Real soldiers love each other." Do you agree or disagree? Why?

5. How difficult is it for you to be transparent? Describe a time when you went out of your way to be transparent.

Locking Arms:

A Man and His Friends, Part 2

How have the mighty fallen in the midst of battle!
Jonathon is slain on your high places.
I am distressed for you, my brother Jonathon....
Your love to me was more wonderful than the love of women.
DAVID TO JONATHON, AFTER GILBOA

I FIRST LEARNED the word *piton* in the same army Ranger school I described in the last chapter. We did some tension climbing, where we would climb on vertical surfaces with nothing above us to pull us up, and with rope fed through snap links. The "piton" is a little anchor bolt. We would find a crack in the wall face, drive this piton into the rock, put the snap link on it, and pass the safety rope through it. That way, we knew we would never fall below that point. We might fall, because we were doing some unbelievable things; but the piton would catch us. We wouldn't fall any further than the anchor in the rock.

So what is a *piton* of friendship? It's a relationship principle that you can count on. It is an anchor bolt in a relationship that will bear your weight, that will hold you up when you find your fingers are slipping. There are other elements in a friendship, of course, but these are basic anchors. You don't want to fall below these levels.

Four Piton Principles of Friendship

Israel faced desperate days in that oppressive year of 1050 B.C. The young kingdom was in pain. Misery. Humiliation. The nation faced harsh military domination by her neighbors, the Philistines. I use that word "neighbor" in the same sense that Iraq was a "neighbor" to Kuwait before the Gulf War and that Nazi Germany was a "neighbor" to Poland before World War II. The Philistines were a coarse people, a militarily strong people. They had bullied and intimidated Israel for years. Backs were bent low. Heads were down. Men passing each other on the dusty roads couldn't meet each others' eyes. The dominance was so strong, Scripture says, that blacksmiths weren't allowed in the country, because the Philistines didn't want any weaponry made.

Israel was helpless in these days. Down and depressed and demoralized and discouraged. Life in the nation was a concentration camp of despair.

Then there was Prince Jonathan.

This young man, the son of King Saul, was an initiator. Masculine to the core. He saw the castdown eyes, slumped shoulders, and drooping heads. He saw all of that, but he still had some hope in his eyes and some fire in his belly. Prince Jonathan believed in the God of Israel. He believed the things he had been taught from childhood about the God of the universe and the God of his people.

Armed with this faith in the living God—and with one of the few swords available in Israel—this young man thought long and hard about taking the initiative. Breaking the stalemate. Giving the Philistines back something of their own. Jonathan had his weapon, all right. Nobody could take it away. If you can't imagine pickpocketing Jim Bowie's knife or sneaking Jesse James's pearl-handled Colt from its holster, don't bother trying to picture a Philistine militia-man walking away with Prince Jonathan's sword.

Circumstances needed to change. Life needed to be different. God's people ought not live in defeat and humiliation. So Jonathan thought through what he might do.

On a given day, armed with this sense of conviction, he and his armor bearer stepped across a line in the sand.

Now the day came that Jonathan, the son of Saul, said to the young man who was carrying his armor, "Come and let us cross over to the Philistines' garrison that is on yonder side" (1 Samuel 14:1).

The prince made his crossing at a little ravine near Michmash.

And between the passes by which Jonathan sought to cross over to the Philistines' garrison, there was a sharp crag on the one side, and a sharp crag on the other side, and the name of the one was Bozez, and the name of the other Seneh. The one crag rose on the north opposite Michmash, and the other on the south opposite Geba. Then Jonathan said to the young man who was carrying his armor, "Come and let us cross over to the garrison of these uncircumcised; perhaps the LORD will work for us, for the LORD is not restrained to save by many or by few." And his armor bearer said to him, "Do all that is in your heart; turn yourself, and here I am with you according to your desire" (vv. 4-7).

Jonathan's masculine heart of steel and initiative shines through. "Perhaps the LORD will work for us, for the LORD is not restrained to save by many or by few." Arithmetic isn't all that critical when God is on your side. His armor bearer doesn't wait for a direct command. "Go for it. Let's do it. I'm your man, heart and soul."

Look at what follows:

And when both of them revealed themselves to the garrison of the Philistines, the Philistines said, "Behold, Hebrews are coming out of the holes where they have hidden themselves." So the men of the garrison hailed Jonathan and his armor bearer and said, "Come up to us and we will tell you something." And Jonathan said to his armor bearer, "Come up after me, for the LORD has given them into the hands of Israel." Then Jonathan climbed up on his hands and feet, with his armor bearer behind him; and they fell before Jonathan, and his armor bearer put some to death after him. And that first slaughter which Jonathan and his armor bearer made was about twenty men within about half a furrow in an acre of land (vv. 11-14).

Can you read into the neat, clean, white spaces between those lines of biblical text? Can you imagine what was happening here? This was hand-to-hand, face-to-face combat. This was muscles tight, teeth clenched, chests heaving, blood splattering, bones snapping, voices yelling, and swords flying. And they did it. Against ten-to-one odds. In one bloody little half-acre of land, overlooking a dry ravine, fighting hand-to-hand in the hot Middle East sun.

When it was all over, two warriors were standing, and twenty Philistine corpses were strewn like rag dolls across the sand. Can you imagine standing there when it was all over, swords and arms and shields dripping with gore? Can you imagine what they must have experienced together in those moments? Smiles? Joyous eye contact? Hugs? Arms locked together, raised to the One who had enabled them?

Just two men left standing, casting long shadows. Jonathan was victorious. It was a great day for him, his armor bearer, and for God's people.

What followed? As you read on in Scripture, it becomes obvious that Jonathan's courage added some fiber to the Israeli army. They stood up straighter. Lifted their eyes. Squared their shoulders. The heart returned to them. They succeeded in rebelling against the Philistine bully boys.

When all the men of Israel who had hidden themselves in the hill country of Ephraim heard that the Philistines had fled, even they also pursued them closely in the battle. So the LORD delivered Israel that day, and the battle spread beyond Beth-aven (vv. 22-23).

The army covered some turf that day because one lone man said to his friend, "Would you go with me? Maybe the Lord will work for us. In fact, I'm sure of it. Let's go climb that cliff and strike a blow for the Lord."

Following this mini-rebellion, Israel enjoyed a few breaths of free air. There were some pleasant days in the land. It was better. All too soon, however, King Saul turned back to his old, careless ways, and the nation once again began to slip away from a courageous walk with God. As a result, they lost His blessing, and the Philistine army rushed back in to fill the vacuum.

By the time you flip over to chapter seventeen, there is absolutely no one to face a Philistine champion in single combat. No one. Not even Jonathan. Not even the plucky prince who had crawled hand over hand up that crag and with a cry of joy and faith took on a whole garrison. When Saul asked for volunteers, Jonathan wasn't there to take a step forward. There's no record of him being the one to stand in the gap against a nine-foot loudmouth named Goliath. Why? Scripture doesn't tell us. But I think it's reasonable to speculate that the valiant prince might have been thinking thoughts such as: *Here we go again. Back under these jokers' thumb. Whining in a corner like scared puppies. How many crags do I have to climb? How many garrisons do I have to fight alone? Why do we always end up here? I can't carry this battle on my shoulders. I just can't do this anymore.*

For the moment, perhaps, Jonathan lost heart. The warrior-prince stepped back into the shadows. But God hadn't run out of heroes.

David spoke to the men who were standing by him saying, "What will be done for the man who kills this Philistine, and takes away the reproach from Israel? For who is this uncircumcised Philistine, that he should taunt the armies of the living God?" (1 Samuel 17:26).

Can't you just hear him, this upstart Jewish kid fresh from the sheep pens? "What's going on here? Who is this big goon? Why is he getting away with that stuff? We're God's people, aren't we? Life shouldn't be like this." It sounds like an echo of Jonathan, doesn't it?

David said to the Philistine, "You come to me with a sword, a spear, and a javelin, but I come to you in the name of the LORD of hosts, the God of the armies of Israel, whom you have taunted. This day the LORD will deliver you up into my hands, and I will strike you down and remove your head from you. And I will give the dead bodies of the army of the Philistines this day to the birds of the sky and the wild beasts of the earth, that all the earth may know that there is a God in Israel" (vv. 45-46).

I don't know where Jonathan's voice had gone, but here was a fresh voice, singing the second verse of the prince's own ballad of courageous faith. It was a faith rooted in the very nature of God.

Apparently it fanned some flames in Jonathan's spirit. David's bravery and white-hot love for God evidently served to draw the prince out of the shadows. As the chapters of 1 Samuel continue, you see a warrior's heart begin beating in the prince's chest once again.

David had stood alone. David had stood strong. David had stood faithful. David had faced the odds. David had taken action. And a disillusioned hero named Jonathan found a friend. Someone that marched to the same tune. The warrior's song that apparently had died in the prince's throat found full voice once again. Only this time, it was a duet.

Note what happens as chapter 17 draws to a close.

Now when Saul saw David going out against the Philistine, he said to Abner the commander of the army, "Abner, whose son is this young man?" And Abner said, "By your life, O king, I do not know." And the king said, "You inquire whose son the youth is." So when David returned from killing the Philistine, Abner took him and brought him before Saul with the Philistine's head in his hand. And Saul said to him, "Whose son are you, young man?" And David answered, "I am the son of your servant Jesse the Bethlehemite."

Now it came about when he had finished speaking to Saul, that the soul of Jonathan was knit to the soul of David, and Jonathan loved him as himself (17:55-18:1).

Jonathan had seen the whole thing. And when David spoke to King Saul, his father, the king's son heard his own heart beating in another man's chest. From that moment, the souls of the two men were knit together.

What a strong statement. Their *souls* were knit. How do souls get knit? Through four piton principles of masculine friendship. Let's look at them, one at a time.

1. Shared values.

You may have many friends in the course of your life, but you will never have a *soul mate* who does not walk with your God. It was David and Jonathan's *souls* that were knit together. The soul is that invisible part of us that combines our minds and wills and emotions. Here were two men whose minds believed the same truth, whose wills locked on to the same course, whose emotions burned at the same injustices.

They were committed to the same God. They loved the same kingdom. They marched to the same tune. They were headed in the same direction. They even dreamed about the same things...a day when their people, their families, their friends, their kingdom could actually live in hope before God.

Now these guys didn't necessarily have the same interests. One was a prince; the other was a shepherd. They didn't necessarily have the same skills or talents or bents. *But they had the same values.* That's at the core of all meaningful friendships, particularly man-to-man. At the core level, at the passion level, at the vision level, they were the same. You don't have to have identical interests or the same kinds of hobbies to be friends.

I have lots of friends here on the staff at Good Shepherd Church, but I'm thinking now of one, Steve, who's probably as different from me as any man in our fellowship. Steve is detail oriented. I don't even know how to spell the word. Steve is competent with numbers. I'm on the verbal side of things. Steve has all daughters. I have all sons. Steve is a specialist with incredible skill. I'm an incurable generalist. Steve is an artist; he can spend hours patiently carving a single piece of wood. I can't even sit still long enough to play a game of tic-tac-toe. We don't have any of the same interests or skills or hobbies or pastimes. *But we are soul mates.* At the VALUES level of our lives, we're walking together step for step. How we want to live well with our wives! How we long to see our children make a difference in a world that's yet to come! We're committed to the same kingdom. We're committed to the same body of Christ. We're committed to the same vision of ministry. He was willing to write off his career in order to be with us here at the church. Our friendship doesn't *require* the same interests or hobbies. It doesn't require listening to the same music, reading the same books, or eating at the same pizza parlor. At the core of who we are, there are shared values. And that is enough.

David and Jonathan both wanted to be part of something that mattered. They wanted to change the way things were where they lived. They wanted to be a part of something bigger than themselves. They owned a flaming desire to serve that greater cause. They wanted to sacrifice together. They wanted to leave a heritage that mattered. They spoke with passion of their futures, their children, and their children's children. They wanted to put their mark on a kingdom, and if necessary to die together for it. Because of their shared values, they were willing to stand together for something much larger than themselves.

That's at the core of friendship. It's much bigger than golf or football. It's much wider and deeper than trout fishing or skiing or woodworking or the Elk's Lodge. It's much more elemental than common interest. It's at the core level of values where we decide we want to do something together no matter what it costs us. That shared dream bonds men together. It's the very essence of meaningful male friendship.

I'm thinking of a scene in the musical, *Les Miserables*. It's in the middle of the French Revolution where a bunch of young men are gathered in a pub the night before a battle. They're students, hardly more than teenagers. But they're part of the Great Revolution, and when daylight comes they must man the barricades. They know they will most likely never see another sunset. And that night...in that little pub...that night before they die together for the principles of the Revolution, they become blood comrades. Brothers. Soul mates. And they sing a song called, "Come Drink with Me." Their song says, in effect, "We're in something bigger than we are and we're in it together. We're willing to pay the price, so we are going to enjoy this last evening together."

Let's sing together. Let's go for it together. Let's die together if that's what it takes. Shared values is at the heart of it all.

2. Unselfish love.

You would have to look long and hard through the pages of scripture—or history—to find a more ringing story of selfless love.

> The soul of Jonathan was knit to the soul of David, and Jonathan loved him as himself.... Then Jonathan made a covenant with David because he loved him as himself. And Jonathan stripped himself of the robe that was on him and gave it to David, with his armor, including his sword and his bow and his belt (1 Samuel 18:1,3-4).

He was saying in effect, "Son of Jesse, I love what I see in your heart. I'm willing to die with you. Everything I have is yours, and I want to be with you. Take it all." Jonathan, in effect, surrendered the very symbols and emblems of his office. He handed them over to a ruddy young warrior out of the hills who dressed in homespun and spoke with a back-country drawl. The two young men were soul mates from that moment. Unselfish love has incredible bonding power.

I'll never forget an incident many years ago when I was in seminary. I found myself carrying a full academic load, holding down three jobs in different parts of the city, and trying to be a husband to Linda and a daddy to two little boys.

We had nothing. We've never been so poor before or since. We subsisted on smelt (tiny migrating fish) friends caught in the rivers and ten-cent packages of green peas from Safeway when they had once-a-month stock-the-freezer sales.

Life was very stressful and times were lean...but I had a desire in my heart to go hunting. One of my last acts before I got out of the military was to buy a rifle. I'd never had one of my own, so I found a good deal, spent a chunk of my final paycheck, and got my gun—knowing it would probably be a decade before I could again afford to get one. I had a friend who knew how much I longed to go hunting and how I needed a break from my busy schedule. So we agreed to go hunting together.

No, there wasn't time, and no, there wasn't money. But we went.

I had been so busy and stressed out and overwhelmed before we left that I hadn't even had time to get my rifle sighted in. But I figured, hey, sighting the rifle—and even finding some game—that's the irrelevant part of hunting. It was just getting out in the woods and being there with a friend that really mattered. So I told him that I didn't have time to sight my rifle, but that it didn't really matter. After all, I laughed, I probably couldn't hit anything even if it *was* sighted correctly.

"It's okay, Stu," he said quietly. "I'll do it for you."

So he took my rifle. It was an old Savage seven-millimeter Remington Magnum with no scope on it, just some open sights. He took it to sight it in. Then, a few days later, we piled into our rigs with our wives and took off.

We took two campers. My dad loaned me his camper, and my friend and his wife took theirs, and we headed over the Cascade Mountains for eastern Oregon to go deer hunting. We arrived at our camp site at ten o'clock on a chilly night. I can't describe how good it felt to be out of the city. The star-strewn sky, the deep quiet, and the fragrance of pine trees and sage brush were like a tonic. Before we hit the sack that night, our friends invited us over to their camper for a steaming mug of hot chocolate—and maybe an Oreo or two.

As I sat down at the little table, my friend said casually, "Oh, by the way, I have your gun here."

He brought out my gun and handed it to me. And there, mounted on it, was a shiny new scope, worth more than the rifle itself. It was completely sighted in. Ready to go. My heart was taken, not because of the value of the gift, but because of the value of the *expression.* That particular gesture at that particular moment in my life hit me in a way I can't easily describe. We became a little more bonded at that point, because he had unselfishly given to me without any fanfare or any big deal. There was no mention of it. It was just something he had wanted to do for me, and that was the end of it. But it wasn't the end of it. John Holmlund's spontaneous act of unselfish love has warmed my heart through long years. I will never forget the act, or the friend. We're still hunting together more than twenty years later.

I want you to notice something else in this David-Jonathan

friendship. Something that *isn't* there. It's conspicuous by its absence. Jonathan stripped himself of his royal robe and gave it to David along with his sword, bow, and belt. What's missing from that picture? What's not there?

Jealousy.

There is none. There is absolutely no competition or comparison between the two men. Jonathan didn't rehearse his inventory of who he was and what he should have. He just yielded his rights and gave generously to his friend. There is no evidence of comparison.

Friends stand by unselfishly, and we draw strength from that.

I have another friend. I don't see him very much anymore, maybe a couple times a year. But over eighteen years ago, he looked me straight in the eyes and made this statement: "Stu, I want you to listen to me a minute. Someday, somewhere, somehow...you're going to need *something* very much. I don't know when. I don't know what. I don't know why. But I *do* know I want you to call me. I will be there."

That's unselfish love. That's a piton principle you can hang your very life on.

3. Deep loyalty.

The plot of this unforgettable saga thickens when Jonathan's father, King Saul, becomes insanely jealous of young David and tries to remove him from the scene.

Now Saul told Jonathan his son and all his servants to put David to death. But Jonathan, Saul's son, greatly delighted in David. So Jonathan told David saying, "Saul my father is seeking to put you to death. Now therefore, please be on guard in the morning and stay in a secret place and hide yourself.... I will speak with my father about you; if I find out anything, then I shall tell you." Then Jonathan spoke well of David to Saul his father, and said to him, "Do not let the king sin against his servant David, since he has not sinned against you, and since his deeds have been very beneficial to you. For he took his life in his hand and struck the Philistine, and the LORD brought about a great deliverance for all Israel; you saw it and rejoiced. Why then will you sin against innocent blood, by putting David to death without a cause?" (1 Samuel 19:1-5).

Jonathan was saying, "You're jealous, Dad. *I'm* the one who should be jealous. I'm the prince, the heir to the throne, and I'm not jealous or intimidated. I'd give my life for this man. Why can't you open your eyes and see that he's on our side?"

Jonathan's loyalty was so deep he was even willing to defend his friend when face-to-face with his father, the king. Loyalty is absolutely essential to a friendship.

Listen to these verses from 1 Samuel 20. Prince Jonathan was speaking to David.

> If it please my father to do you harm, may the LORD do so to Jonathan and more also, if I do not make it known to you and send you away, that you may go in safety. And may the LORD be with you as He has been with my father. And if I am still alive, will you not show me the lovingkindness of the LORD, that I may not die? And you shall not cut off your lovingkindness from my house forever, not even when the LORD cuts off every one of the enemies of David from the face of the earth (vv. 13-15).

Could our friendship live through the generations, David? Even when it's going great for you, when the Lord has done for you all that's in His heart to do, will you remember me? Will you remember my kids after I'm gone?"

And Jonathan made David vow again because of his love for him, because he loved him as he loved his own life (v. 17).

Have you ever said something like this to a friend? "My wife and I have talked about it and we would really be honored—if something ever happened to us—if you would raise our children." You need to consider making that a part of your legal will. What a comfort to hear loyal friends say, "If anything would happen to you and your wife, we'd be honored to have your children. We'd be honored to be part of your future. Our friendship will live through the generations. Let's get it in writing."

Loyalty is something you *express*. You say it out loud. You write it down. It isn't just "understood" in some vague sort of way; it is expressed in a vow, in a covenant, in a promise, in a conversation man-to-man. We need to learn to express it: a complete and total loyalty that says, "You are my brother."

After the death of Hollywood great, Jack Benny, fellow entertainer George Burns had these words to say about his long-time friend. "Jack and I had a wonderful friendship for nearly fifty-five years. Jack never walked out on me when I sang a song, and I never walked out on him when he played the violin. We laughed together. We worked together. We ate together. I suppose that for many of those years, we talked every single day."[1]

A man-to-man friendship says, I'll never walk out on you. Barring unrepentant sin against the Lord God, you'll never be able to do anything that will repulse me or break our fellowship.

4. Real transparency.

We spoke of this "piton" briefly in the previous chapter. There can be no soul-level friendship without it. In 1 Samuel 20:3, David spoke his heart again, saying:

> Your father knows well that I have found favor in your sight, and he has said, "Do not let Jonathan know this, lest he be grieved." But truly as the LORD lives and as your soul lives, there is hardly a step between me and death.

In verse 9, Jonathan replies, "Far be it from you! For if I should indeed learn that evil has been decided by my father to come upon you, then would I not tell you about it?" Implication? *Of course I would!*

Verse 41 tells us that "David rose from the south side and fell on his face to the ground, and bowed three times. And they kissed each other and wept together, but David more."

I'll never forget when my brother experienced a season of separation from his lovely and loving wife. Today you would never know that they'd been through those kinds of waters, but there were twenty months early in their marriage when they didn't live together. I remember my brother coming and staying with us at our home. I don't even remember how long it was, but it wasn't long enough. I wouldn't trade those months of closeness and sharing for anything. I remember crying together. I remember rubbing our beards together as we cried. I'd never hugged my brother like that before. I'll never forget it. I don't think he will either.

David and Jonathan were not ashamed to embrace and weep together. They were that genuine with one another. They were that unconcerned with their "image." They expressed their emotions with utter and total transparency.

It was Jesus who said, in effect, to his men: "You know, I used to call you all slaves. I used to call you all servants. I'm not going to do that anymore. I'm going to call you friends, because friends know what's going on with each other. And I'm going to include you in the know" (see John 15:15).

What defines our friendship is the telling of ourselves. The revealing of emotions.

David Smith, author of *The Friendless American Male*, writes,

Very early in life, little boys receive the cultural message that they're not supposed to show emotions. Expressing feelings is generally a taboo for males. Boys soon learn to dread the words, "Don't be a sissy; Big boys don't cry; Aren't you a little too old to be sitting on your daddy's lap?" Other messages come through loud and clear—Boys have to learn to be men. And to be a man means you conceal your emotions.[2]

Boys do need to learn to be men. But being a man does not mean concealing your emotions. Part of being a man is real transparency. It's also a piton principle of friendship.

John Powell's classic book, *Why Am I Afraid to Tell You Who I Am?* walks us through some of the degrees of transparency that we need to be alert to. When we're communicating with our friends, there are at least five levels of communication. The cliché level is little more than elevator talk. It's a quick "How ya doin'?" without really waiting for the answer. It's a "Whaddya think about this weather?" when you really don't care. The degree of transparency in this sort of communication is

"Be on the alert. Stand firm in the faith. Act like men. Be strong. Let all that you do be done in love."

THE APOSTLE PAUL
Spring, A.D. 54

practically nil. You can have an exchange like this with total strangers. In fact, this kind of empty chatter serves as a protective relational buffer that *keeps* people total strangers.

Then there's the fact level of communication, which is sharing what you know. The degree of transparency is a little more real, but it's still the kind of talk that you can engage in with just about anyone. Do you remember "Dragnet," the old television series? The hard-bitten police lieutenant, Joe Friday, was always interrupting some lady's woeful recitation of her miseries with the monotone line, "Just the facts, ma'am." Facts are the hallmark of this level of conversation. And while facts reveal what you know, they do little to reveal who you are. This sort of talk holds people at arm's length. It doesn't let them in.

Next comes the **opinion level** of communication. This is sharing what you *think*. You're starting to let a little bit of yourself out, but you're still keeping people at a "safe" distance. Yes, there are fewer people you can communicate with on this level, but you really can't build a relationship on opinions. Friendship has to go deeper than that.

When you finally get to the **emotional and transparent levels** of communication, you are actually sharing *who you are*. The degree of transparency greatly increases and the number of people with whom you can share is much smaller. The levels of trust and commitment and bonding take a dramatic upward curve on the friendship chart. That kind of sharing makes for much deeper and stronger relationships.

Emotional communication means conveying hopes and fears and dislikes and aspirations and disappointments and sorrows. It's giving away who you are. It's giving away a part of yourself.

Sometimes we're not very good at this sort of thing because of a false concept of manhood and pride which prevents us from sharing our feelings. Or maybe we have a warped view of spirituality that says, *If I was really a good Christian, I wouldn't feel this way.* That's pure bunk, of course. The New Testament brims with exhortations to humble ourselves, speak truthfully, and to encourage one another along this sometimes bumpy road called "the Christian life."

We need to practice sharing our emotions with other men. So it isn't easy. So what? Who ever said that growth *was* easy? Kent Hughes writes:

Men, if you're married, your wife must be your most intimate friend, but to say "my wife is my best friend" can be a cop-out. You also need Christian male friends who have a same-sex understanding of the serpentine passages of your heart who will not only offer counsel and pray for you, but will also hold you accountable to your commitments and responsibilities when necessary.[3]

I'll never forget the day, maybe twenty years ago, when my friend interrupted me midsentence. There was steel in his eyes as he looked right into mine. His words were, *"Why don't you just DO IT. It's your JOB as his father."* It was a confrontive statement, and it stung…for the moment. Nevertheless, because he was my friend, I had given him the right to say it. His words struck deep and strong, and it made a change in my life.

Transparency is very real, very powerful. When you practice it with a true friend, you will find that friend increasingly drawn to you rather than repulsed. The reason we *don't* tell people what we feel is because we're afraid they won't like us. Yet Scripture says that every temptation you face, every sin you struggle with, every liability that curses your life *is common to man.* We all struggle with the same things, to one degree or another. So everything that's killing you is somewhere in the chest of every man you know. The Bible also says that everything you have that's an asset, an encouragement, a positive trait, *is a gift from God.* Those things being true, none of us have anything to brag or boast about. None of us has anything to feel cast down or destroyed about that is not common to man.

So here we have four principles of friendship. Four principles hammered into the rocky face of daily life. Drive them in deep, Tender Warriors. You never know when you might lose your grip. You never know when you might fall. Real friendship will keep you from hitting the bottom.

A Man Faces Himself

1. Plan a two- or three-day experience with your closest friends—such as camping, fishing, something you enjoy. Make your specific objective (around the fire?) to clarify your shared core values. Determine how you can encourage each other to practice and strengthen them.

2. Take some time out this week to let your closest friend know how much you value his loyalty, transparency, unselfish love, and core values. Make it explicit to him what you admire.

A Man Meets with His Friends

1. Evaluate the statement, "Arithmetic isn't all that critical when God is on your side"? Describe a time when you acted on this principle.

2. Do you have a male friend whose soul is knit to your own? If so, how did it get that way? How did the friendship blossom?

3. Since core values are critical to intimate friendship, have you determined what your core values are? List them.

4. How do you show unselfish love to your closest friend(s)? What act of unselfish love on the part of a close friend has meant a great deal to you?

5. How do you recognize deep loyalty in a friend? How do you know when it's absent? How do you develop it in yourself?

6. Do you have at least one male friend with whom you can be completely transparent? If so, how did the transparency develop? If not, what can a man do to find and develop such a friend?

7. How much time do you spend with close friends discussing matters that matter—things that touch the heart as well as eternity? When you have such discussions, what topics come up? What topics do you wish came up more often?

CHAPTER FOURTEEN

The Ultimate Tender Warrior:

A Man and His Lord

*And He died for all, that those who live should no longer live for themselves but
for Him who died and rose again on their behalf*
(2 CORINTHIANS 5:15).

ONE OF THE CHOICEST snapshots in my mental album
dates from a moment when I was half a world away from the
event.

It happened over two decades ago while I was slogging through
the deltas and jungles of Southeast Asia. My father was playing the
role with my one-year-old son that I would have loved to have been
playing. Little Kent and his grandpa were wrestling and rolling
around on the carpet like grandpas and grandsons are supposed to do.
In the course of all that thrashing about, one of Kent's fingers inadver-
tently scratched my father's eye. It didn't hurt much, but Dad decided
to take advantage of the situation and appeal to this little one. Down
on his knees, Dad dropped his head to the floor and buried his face in
the carpet. He covered the sides of his face with his hands and began
howling and carrying on, as if in great distress.

Little Kent, however, had already picked up a few things about
life. In a life span of twelve months, he'd begun to learn something
about grandpas—and men. So he got down on the carpet as close as

he could to his grandpa's face. He kept trying to pull those big hands away from the hidden face so he could look into his grandpa's eyes.

"Aw, Bompa," my boy said. "Be a *big* Bompa."

Kent knew something about Bompas. About big men. About strong men. He had some expectations. His grandpa was a grown man, and Kent was expecting something of him. My little guy was already becoming alert to the masculine qualities of strength and courage. And in his one-year-old owning of this thing called "masculinity," he was trying to impart courage to another human being.

Come on, Bompa. Be a big Bompa. Big Bompas can take the rough and tumble. Big Bompas can absorb the hits and bounce back. Big Bompas are supposed to be strong, stable, and provide direction...not whine around on the carpet.

What Does It Mean to Be a Man?

Joe Stowell, president of Moody Bible Institute, writes, "I was born male. But early in my life, I learned that being male did not necessarily make me a *man*. I realized this the first time somebody said, 'Joe, be a man.' It was probably when I had started crying or refused to eat my spinach. I discovered that I had a new task in life: to go beyond just being a male and discover what it meant to be a 'man.'"[1]

As we approach the last few steps of this little journey together, let's fill our vision with another young Man, learning to be what He was meant to be.

And the Child continued to grow and become strong, increasing in wisdom; and the grace of God was upon Him.

And His parents used to go to Jerusalem every year at the Feast of the Passover. And when He became twelve, they went up there according to the custom of the Feast; and as they were returning, after spending the full number of days, the boy Jesus stayed behind in Jerusalem. And His parents were unaware of it, but supposed Him to be in the caravan, and went a day's journey; and they began looking for Him among their relatives and acquaintances. And when they did not find Him, they returned to Jerusalem, looking for Him. And it came about that after three days they found Him in the temple, sitting in the midst of the teachers, both listening to them, and asking them questions. And all who heard Him were amazed at His understanding and His answers. And when they saw Him, they were astonished; and His mother said to Him, "Son, why have You treated us this way? Behold, Your father and I have been anxiously looking for You."

And He said to them, "Why is it that you were looking for Me? Did you not know that I had to be in My Father's house?" (Luke 2:40-49).

A modified King James Version might render that last line, "Didn't you know I had to be about My Father's business?"

Jesus was a boy beginning to assert His calling. He was fast becoming a man. He was fast living out what He was for. He was saying to Mary and Joseph, in essence, "Why are you surprised? Why would you be looking for Me anywhere else? Don't you know I was born for this? This is who I am, this is what I do. Is that so surprising to you?"

There was a sense of destiny about this twelve-year-old.

It's an inner equilibrium increasingly hard to find among the boys and men of our culture. Some time ago I found myself watching a local audience-participation television talk show. I normally would have flipped the channel—quickly. But when I heard them talking about the emerging men's movement, I sat back to listen. I had read about Robert Bly's "gathering of men" and had seen Bill Moyer's treatment of the phenomenon in a PBS documentary. But that program had dealt only with the big guns of the movement. It was carried off with slick professionalism. Cutaways and overspeaks at all the right moments. And the men who spoke with Moyers sounded impressive and intelligent.

This local program was a different matter. Less professional. Painfully unrehearsed. Closer to home. A small market, in-studio production. No big-name kahunas or distinguished, gray-maned gurus. No obvious leader or spokesman. The audience was all male, most of whom had attended men's gatherings. These were the disciples. The followers. The little guys. *Now*, I told myself, *I'll get to see the local, unedited, unvarnished product of the movement.*

I was expectant. But what I saw shocked and disappointed me.

I had expected to see men. Exhilarated men. Men happy to be men. Men enthused to be about their business—whatever it was. But what I saw looked more like the ragged remnants of a recovery program. I felt compassion for them. These fellows sounded like members of a local mental health group. Each seemed to be looking for something missing. There wasn't a Big Bompa in the whole lot.

It occurred to me that for all the bravado—getting naked, beating drums, passing the "talking stick," whatever—this was nothing more than a group of despondent baby-boomers commiserating with each other. What they had found was not "a gathering of men," but a male therapy group.

The program's producer said it all when he flashed one graphic on the screen as he cut away to a commercial. It was a quote from Mark Twain:

"Deep down in his heart, no man respects himself."

Is that true? The line certainly seemed to describe the audience in Studio B that afternoon.

As the program limped to a conclusion, I asked Linda, "Did you see any men in that audience?" What I had seen was a group of unhappy human beings, and my heart went out to them. But I had not seen any men. I found myself asking the question, "What's missing from this picture?" It looked like the seventies all over again. Only this time it wasn't a "lost generation," it was a "lost gender."

"Is there something wrong with me?" I asked Linda. "I'm a man. I want to be with men. But there is no one in that entire group that I'm drawn to. No one I would care to spend time with."

These were men looking for themselves. Men adrift. I pictured a vessel with no prow, no stern, no rudder, and—worse yet—*no keel.* I pictured everyone with an oar in the water, paddling here and there. Solemnly going around and around in circles. Going nowhere at all, and despising every moment of the fruitless journey.

Where do you go to find the keel of manhood? Where do you go to find the rudder with which to steer your masculinity? Where do you find the zenith, the epitome of manliness?

Joe Stowell asks:

What does it mean to be a man? Society presents us with the macho Marlboro man, the mild-mannered sensitive man, the suave artsy man, the Monday night football man, the cunning marketplace man who moves through the corporate stream like a shark.

These contrasting portraits make many of us feel insecure about our manhood. There always seems to be a better athlete or more successful businessman. There is always someone who is slimmer, trimmer, and tougher than we are.

When we are rejected by women, these insecurities surface painfully. (Remember how you felt when the first girl you asked out said no?) When confronted by family pressures or marketplace sharks, we feel intimidated. Our cultural environment compounds the problem, making some of us feel almost ashamed of our masculinity.[2]

Look to Jesus for the Model

Where do you go to look for that masculinity? There are all kinds of false models out there. Where is the Real? I suggest what should already be obvious.

Jesus Christ is the ultimate Man. Maximum manhood. The perfect Model. The complete Hero.

Why is it that when someone says, "Picture the archetypal male," the image that comes to mind is *not* one of Jesus? Why is that? I have to confess that, for years, the picture in my mind would not have been Jesus. It wouldn't have occurred to me. Why? I think it's because we've looked in all the wrong places for our images of manhood. We've allowed our vision of Jesus to be truncated by a media that either hates and distorts Him or vastly misunderstands Him. We've developed our images of the God-man in the darkrooms of the uncaring and uninformed.

Even the single most famous portrait of Jesus makes Him look more like a pouting model for Breck shampoo than a man. Doesn't it? His eyes aren't toward you. The face is thin and aloof. The long hair is waved and feminine.

Hollywood seems consistently to portray Jesus Christ as some kind of space cadet. His eyes are never quite focused. His mind is never quite engaged with reality. He's always halfway between here and Somewhere Else. His mysticism is so spooky and other-worldly that He can't be real. He is unreal and therefore irrelevant. And that's not the Jesus of the Bible. Somehow we've allowed Him to be painted as "gentle Jesus meek and mild" or "the pale Galilean." He is so much more than those images. He is very real. Forever relevant. And if I read the Bible correctly, fully human.

My visual picture of Christ's masculinity changed forever when I visited Israel for the first time in 1974. The Breck shampoo ads fell off my mental screen when we stepped off the plane and met David (pronounced DaVEED), the driver for our group. I watched David for nine weeks. He was a twenty-five-year-old Jewish male in his prime, a native-born *sabra.* That's the modern Hebrew term for a prickly pear cactus: tough on the outside, tender and sweet within. David's skin was dark. Dark by pigment, dark by the bronzing of the sun. His hair was black, medium length, somewhat wavy. It hung naturally on his head and matted on his forehead in the afternoon heat.

More than anything else, I noticed his eyes. Very dark. Sometimes hard as black steel, sometimes soft, with smiles dancing on the edges. Piercing eyes. Kind eyes. Intelligent eyes. Eyes brimming with life.

David was so serious and so hilarious all at the same time that we were irresistibly drawn to him. He had just been released from the hospital, where he had been convalescing from wounds suffered in the Yom Kippur war. I'll never forget the picture he made as he first stood before us…clad in neat khakis, arms folded, legs apart, smiling a welcome. In love with life, in love with his family, in love with his people and nation.

As we became acquainted, my mind was drawn back to another "Daveed," three thousand years previous, from the same gene pool.

That David had been a great warrior. The complete Hebrew man of his day. In love with life, his family, his nation, and his God. From that David, it wasn't much of a mental jump to cross a thousand years to the greater Son of David, Jesus of Nazareth, the ultimate King, Warrior, Mentor, and Friend.

Three men, all with the same sense of origin. All from the same covenant people. Without consciously trying to adjust the mental image, I found myself thinking differently of Jesus. The pale, limp-wristed Galilean faded like a bad dream and the laughing, dark-skinned Son of David took over the picture in my mind. The Greater *Sabra*. The real Tender Warrior.

Again, Joe Stowell speaks for me when he says:

Many of us fear that…if we fully yield the reins of our life to Christ, He will take away our manhood. Victims of a demas-culinized portrait of Christ, we have forgotten that His perfect blend of divinity and humanity was expressed through exis-tence as a man. He was the perfect expression of manhood. While that meant He had a special compassionate side, He also displayed strength and power. Enough strength and power to attract strong men as His followers. Enough so that they even gave up their careers and personal ambitions and followed Him.

Jesus Christ does not at all diminish our manhood. He emerges through the distinct qualities of our maleness to cre-ate a fuller and richer expression of what a man can be.

He redefines our manhood by replacing the motivations of our world with new guidelines for success. He directs our manhood along the path of ultimate significance. He takes our instincts to protect, provide, conquer, and accumulate, and points them in productive directions.[3]

The Heart of Jesus' Manhood: Purpose

As you consider the life of Jesus, what singular, overarching char-acteristic describes His thirty-three years on our planet? What overrid-ing, all-encompassing trait says, "That's Jesus"? Yes, there are many adjectives that accurately describe His person. Loving, caring, strong, pure, powerful, gentle, firm, unselfish, kind. But larger than those depictions of His attributes, what lone virtue would you use to describe Him?

I think we saw it when, as a boy of twelve, He said, "Mom, why would you have looked for Me anywhere else? I have to be about My Father's business."

There was a sense of purpose in Jesus. A clarity of vision. A force of direction. Everything that I *didn't* see in the men's TV talk show is the singular, preeminent characteristic of the ultimate Man.

Men today are searching. That's obvious. But all the searching in the world is no good if you're not looking in the right place. Those men in the televised "gathering," sincere as they might have been, were still very much without resolve. They were still asking, "What makes a man? Who am I? What do I do?"

Conspicuous by its absence was a sense of purpose. No vision shimmered on the horizon. No mountain peaks called from the purple distance. No steely convictions glinted in the eyes. There was only confusion and mist. The soft fog of "self-talk" with neither direction nor resolution.

The single thing that marks every aspect of Jesus' life was a driving sense of cause. "THIS is who I am, THIS is what I do, THIS is where I am going...*and why don't you come, too?*" He was a man on a mission. That's what swept strong men along in His wake. That's what persuaded them in a heartbeat to drop their fishing nets or hammers or ledgers or whatever else they were doing and follow Him. Suddenly whatever had preoccupied them seemed pallid and tame and slightly irrelevant. The Man who called them was a burning Reality. A Great Light. How could they help but saddle up and trail along?

A real man knows where he is going.

Dr. Luke offers this revealing snapshot in chapter 9 of his gospel.

And it came about, when the days were approaching for His ascension, that He resolutely set His face to go to Jerusalem.... He was journeying with His face toward Jerusalem (Luke 9:51,53).

He set His face. He locked His eyes. He cemented His direction. He was going somewhere. He owned an unshakable purpose. He set His face to go to Jerusalem, knowing full well what faced Him there. Hatred and ridicule and torture and the unspeakable sin and rebellion of all the world for all time seared into His being. Blacker by far than any of these shadows, He faced the rejection and white-hot wrath of His own Father. But even those prospects did not slow His feet or weaken His resolve. He was willing to pay the ultimate price because He was a man on a mission.

In John 19:30, we see the final, blinding burst of that flaming resolve. This time, the God-man was hanging on a cross. To those around Him, He looked like a victim. He was anything but a victim. Submerged as He was in a sea of pain and horror, He was so alert to the tiny particulars of Scripture that He whispered "I thirst," to the soldiers who gazed at Him from below. The vinegar found its way to His parched lips, and when that was done, having accomplished it all, He cried out with a loud voice, "It is finished!"

It wasn't a whimper. It wasn't a sigh of resignation. It was a shout of triumph that shook the cosmos from the dungeons of hell to the corona of Alpha Centauri.

"IT'S DONE!"

And so it was. The mission was completed. He had accomplished what He had come to do. He had wrapped up His Father's business.

A few hours earlier, anticipating that moment, He had lifted His eyes to heaven and said, "I have accomplished the work You have given Me to do."

That's the heart of what makes a man. That ringing sense of destiny. That soul-seizing challenge to overcome. To conquer for a cause.

A Real Man Must Have a Cause Outside Himself

A man, you see, was made for a cause. A man was made for something outside of himself. A man was made for something beyond. That's why so many of us draw a disproportionate sense of achievement from our jobs, ordinary as they may be. And that's why so many newly-retired men suddenly find life tasteless and empty. Through all their years, they have completely attached their masculine identity to the Wedgewood Lumber Company or the Pushpenny National Bank or the Western Widget Consortium. Then, when they have worked their thirty or forty years and collected their gold watch, it's done. Their job is over, and so is their reason for living! What is left to do but tuck your watch in the top drawer, lie in your bed, draw up your legs, and die?

What a prostitution of the image of God in man! What a needless tragedy! For the cause of Christ *never* dies. Never lessens its call on a man's life. Never ceases to throb with urgency as time rushes on a short track toward eternity.

The cause is eternal.

The kingdom is out there.

Kingdom deeds await doing in the borrowed might of the Almighty.

If you and I keep trying to attach our purpose for living to some work-a-day profession or nine-to-five job, we forfeit the heart of true masculinity. *No wonder* so many of us become frustrated in our careers and find ourselves on the canyon rim of life crises. No wonder we find ourselves numbed at times by the crushing emptiness of it all. We're looking for purpose; we were made for a purpose, and our puny jobs just aren't *big* enough to slake that thirst.

What do you see, after all, when you look at the vehicle of a man's physical body? What was it made for? Check it out. In contrast, what does a woman's body tell you a woman was made for? Every twenty-eight days or so her body tells her she was made for life and its sustenance. Her breasts remind her that she was made for giving life and nurturing life. What does a man's body tell you? Not a thing! Why? Because the purpose for a man is out on the horizon. A man was made to be a provisionary, a wagon scout, out there in front, looking ahead. The purpose isn't inside. And if we spend all our time beating drums and self-talking and staring at our navels, we're never going to find real manhood.

We must find that purpose outside of ourselves.

We must find it in Him.

That's why Paul, who focused his very life around that purpose and vision, could say, "For to me, to live, is Christ." That's it. That's who I am. That's what I'm for. That's why I'm here. That's why I endure everything I have to endure. Life isn't only *in* Jesus, life IS Jesus. Then, at the end of it all, in a dank dungeon on Rome's death row, he wrote to his young Ranger Buddy,

> The time of my departure has come. I have fought the good fight, I have finished the course, I have kept the faith (2 Timothy 4:6-7).

There was no fading into obscurity for the warrior from Tarsus. No sitting on a shopping mall bench watching the world go by. No endless games of shuffleboard. He left life with a cry of joy and fulfillment. "I have finished!" That's what God wants to be normative for all of His men.

A couple of years ago my brother, Eric, told me of a painting that had grabbed his heart. He said, "Stu, you have to see this. It's going to grip you." I finally saw that piece of art last spring, hanging on the wall of a friend's home.

He was right; it did grip me.

I found myself, along with several other men in the room, staring and staring at that painting. It's the kind of picture that requires staring. It's the kind of painting that calls for pondering, reflection, and projecting one's self into the image, to see if there is a fit.

It's a picture of four men riding. Horsemen. Riding together. Riding straight at you. James Dobson reproduced the painting on the cover of *Focus on the Family* magazine. It looked good on a nine-by-twelve inch magazine cover, but it looks better full-sized, gracing a big wall. There's so much to see. What was it that appealed to us as we stood there, experiencing that picture together? Some reflection of the Marlboro man out there in the back country? Hardly. The Marlboro man always rode alone. He was an independent type, out there by and for himself. These men weren't of that stripe at all.

What was it about that picture? I can tell you what I saw. These clear-eyed riders had tamed the beasts beneath them…and within them. They were riding together as comrades. Not alone. Not isolated.

They had understood that masculinity was made for connection. They rode together upstream. Fully equipped to face the elements. You could see their breath on the cold fall morning. They rode together as friends and soul-mates and warriors, against the force of the current, into the cold wind and *exhilarating* in it.

But there's more to it. There's a story behind it. Those men were going somewhere. There was something out there, ahead of them, beyond them. They were men on a mission. They were going for it with everything in them.

That's what struck us—an image of men with a *calling*. Carried along by something beyond themselves. Willing to face the obstacles. Willing to buck the current and the wind and the dangers. Willing to die, if necessary.

Focus on the Family commissioned that painting to commemorate four men who were key to that organization. They were killed in a plane crash on their way home from a ministry retreat. Four laymen protecting—through their ministry involvement—the spiritual values of a whole nation. Four men who were teaching through life and words the principles of the living God—lived out in their homes and their neighborhoods. Four men who were loving and caring for their own and beyond their own. Men who were other-oriented, not self-oriented. Men on a mission paying the price.

That's the overarching characteristic of Christ's life. He was a man on a mission. A mission that mattered forever. And until you and I orient ourselves to the calling of Christ, we will never truly be men.

That's what caused Him to stay focused and locked in when everything in His humanity cried in His ears to spare Himself and turn aside. With a voice torn by grief, He said, "Father, if there's no other way, then not My will but Yours be done." He submitted to the purpose, calling, will, and vision of His Father. And so can we.

Men, you and I need to own for ourselves that same clarity of vision that so marked the life of Christ. We need to give ourselves up for our brides and *the* Bride as He did. So that the family might be healthy. So that the people might live well. So that this nation might continue to experience His favor and remain the land of the free.

There are some little guys and gals out there who need Big Bompas.

There are some women out there who need clear-eyed provisionaries. Men who face the worst hell has to throw at them and stay and stay and stay.

There's a world out there that needs some Tender Warriors.

It's every man's purpose…every woman's dream…and every child's hope. It's the definition of a man. I want to head down that road with all my heart. But I want some Ranger Buddies to walk with me. Will you come? Let's do it together.

A Man Faces Himself

1. Read through the Gospel of Mark as quickly as you can, in a single sitting if possible. What impression do you get of the "manliness" of Jesus Christ? Try the same thing in the other Gospels as well. In what specific ways is His manliness a challenge to your own?

2. Take a good long look at your relationship with Christ. What kind of priority does it have? Consider asking your wife and your pastor to make the same evaluation of you. Make necessary adjustments. It matters.

A Man Meets with His Friends

1. Has anyone ever told you to "be a man"? What did he or she mean? How did you react?

2. What would you say is your calling in life?

3. What do you think of Mark Twain's statement: "Deep down in his heart, no man respects himself"?

4. Describe your own mental picture of Jesus Christ.

5. If a hidden observer were to study your actions for thirty days, what conclusions would he make about your purpose in life? Where would he say you were going?

6. Do you have a cause which gives your life meaning? If so, what is it? How does it affect your day-to-day living? If it doesn't, why not?

7. How closely do you identify with the apostle Paul's words, "For to me, to live, is Christ"?

8. Now that you have read *Tender Warrior*, how would you describe a "man's man"?

Where Do We Go from Here?

OKAY TENDER WARRIORS, just where do we go from here? How about church? Go to church? Precisely! That's an excellent idea. After all, what really matters? Two things. Two things only—your family and His family. Both require strong commitment.

Whether it's on a wagon train winding its way across the prairie, a muddy hillside in Vietnam, or in a household in America, you and I need to lead those around us to follow His lead. And that means we will do nothing alone. We will walk in a great company. It's called church. We'll talk more about that in a minute. For now, let me toss you a couple of preliminary thoughts. Let's do what any maturing human being does—*stop*, *look*, and *listen*.

Climb the tallest tree you can find. Get a good look at the sweep of sky and landmarks around you. Get some perspective. The first thing to do is...

Stop

Stop hanging around, taking up space, and eating groceries. Stop going to work to support a lifestyle. Stop living for weekends. Reorganize your priorities. Stop missing out on your family. And if you're into pornography—society's greatest mankiller—*stop* that, too. Where do we go from here? Someplace other than where we've been. We have to stop some things and get on with others.

Look

Are you up in that tree, yet? Scanning the horizon? Look at what's available to you. There are all kinds of tools out there to help you strengthen your manhood. The fact that you are reading this book means you're alert to reading. Read some more. READ. Then re-read again. Spend some money to get the very best resources.

Listen

Listen to those who have proved themselves. Big men in tall places who are faithful—Jim Dobson, Chuck Swindoll, Dennis Rainey, Charles Stanley, to name four sturdy horsemen of the Word. When you're on that freeway in the morning, tune in! You can get the sports and weather and all the bad news you can digest in your newspaper at night. Reserve your commute for good news.

Then Go!

You have a big green light. Let your wheels and your heart and your momentum move you back to God's people. Back to church.

Yeah, you're right. There *is* a lot of baloney out there that passes for church. Just don't worry about that stuff. Forget about it...and find the real thing. Because *that's* out there, too! How do you know a real church when you see one? Let me offer a few clues, as we pack our warbags and get ready to walk out the back door of this book.

Find a Church That...

1. Takes God and His Word Seriously. We might call it a teaching church. This kind of church believes the Bible is indeed God's Word. His inerrant Word. Scripture is not something to be trifled with. It is the *only* standard for this church's faith and practice. This church is not overly absorbed and enamored with some pastor or other individual who may be greatly gifted, impressive, or full of charisma. In fact, most churches that take God's Word seriously appreciate the breadth of gifts in the body, and enjoy a team approach to ministry. Men were created to walk together. To play team ball. This is a church that works hard at expounding Scripture and seeing it *applied* to daily living.

2. *Takes You Seriously.* This is a church that looks long and hard at all God has wrapped in you—the unique blend of passions, interests, gifts, talents, and visions that you are—and harnesses them for the kingdom. So that you and other Tender Warriors can be all God intended you to be. So that you and other Tender Warriors can pull together like true yokefellows, plowing a straight line toward the realization of God's rule "on earth as it is in heaven." This is a church that has some expectations of you—biblical expectations—and it will help you take a good look at yourself and your unique contribution to the Body of Christ and "God's plan of the ages."

3. *Takes Itself Seriously.* This church might be called an *equipping* church. It sees its mission as providing you with the tools you need to live the kind of life God called you to live. This church's pastoral staff sees itself as a coaching staff. Such a church will move you off the bench, onto the playing floor, and stretch you beyond simple "spectatorship." Most of us have had enough of "riding the pines." We need to get into the only game that matters. In the words of that ancient warrior, Paul, this church will equip you to "do the work of the ministry."

If it doesn't have one already, this church will probably be moving toward developing an effective ministry to men, a meat-and-potatoes effort to call men to God's design for manhood. It's a fellowship that works hard at building kings, warriors, mentors, and friends. And it will help you find a couple of Ranger Buddies with whom you can lock arms. You may even find yourself going to breakfast with some guys, penetrating hearts, and loving it.

Start your journey with the application questions at the end of each chapter in this book.

And welcome to the communion of Tender Warriors!

For conference or speaking information contact Stu Weber at:
Stu Weber
2229 N.E. Burnside, #212
Gresham, Oregon 97030

Chapter 2

1. Erma Bombeck, *Family—The Ties That Bind...and Gag!* (New York: Fawcett Crest, 1987), 2-3.

2. Max Lucado, *God Came Near* (Portland, Ore.: Multnomah Press, 1987), 161.

Chapter 3

1. Robert Bly, *Iron John* (New York: Vintage Books, 1992), x-xi. Copyright 1990 by Robert Bly.

2. Robert Moore and Douglas Gillette, *King Warrior, Magician, Lover* (San Francisco: Harper, 1990), 9.

3. Elisabeth Elliot, *The Mark of a Man* (Old Tappan, N.J.: Revel, 1981), 51.

Chapter 4

1. Weldon Hardenbrook, *Missing from Action* (Nashville: Thomas Nelson, Inc., 1987), 82.

2. As quoted in Ibid.

3. David Elkind, "Youngsters Under Stress—What Parents Do," *U.S. News & World Report,* 9 August 1982, 58. (As cited in Ibid.)

4. John Leo, "A Family Plan for Uncle Sam," *U.S. News & World Report,* 30 November 1992, 22.

5. Lewis Smedes, "The Power of Promising," *Christianity Today,* 21 January 1983, 16-17.

6. Hardenbrook, *Missing from Action,* 128-129.

Chapter 5

1. Robert Bly, *Iron John* (New York: Vintage Books, 1992), 2-3. Copyright 1990 by Robert Bly.

2. From Stu: "I've seen this statement from Vince Lombardi on desk tops, office walls, and slips of paper in wallets, but I've never been able to locate its original source."

Chapter 6

1. Lisa Schlein, *Atlanta Journal,* January 1988, 2. As quoted by Robert Lewis and William Hendricks, *Rocking the Roles* (Colorado Springs: Navpress, 1991), 59.

2. Elisabeth Elliot, *The Mark of a Man* (Old Tappan: Fleming H. Revell, 1981), 44-45.

3. Stephen B. Clark, *Man and Woman in Christ* (Ann Arbor, Mich.: Servant Books, 1980), 413.

4. Sherry Ortner as quoted in Ibid., 423.

5. Sherry B. Ortner, "Is female to male as nature is to culture?" *Women, Culture, & Society*, ed. M. Rosaldo and L. Lamphere (Stanford Varsity Press, 1974). As quoted by Ibid., 414.

Chapter 7

1. Joyce Brothers, *What Every Woman Should Know about Men* (New York: Simon and Schuster, 1981), 11-13.

2. Ibid.

3. Paul Popenoe, "Are Women Really Different?" *Family Life*, February 1971.

4. Data gathered by Richard Restak, neurologist at Georgetown University School of Medicine. As quoted in Family Life Marriage Conference manual, 113-114.

5. Anastasia Toufexis, "Coming from a Different Place," *Time* (special edition), Fall 1990, 65.

6. Ibid.

7. Christine Gorman, "Sizing Up the Sexes," *Time*, 20 January 1992, 42.

8. Gary Smalley, *The Joy of Committed Love* (Grand Rapids: Zondervan, 1984), 179.

9. Ibid.

Chapter 8

1. Richard Halverson, *No Greater Power* (Portland, Ore.: Multnomah Press, 1986), 118.

2. James Dobson, *Straight Talk* (Dallas: Word, 1991), 180-181.

3. Ibid., 181.

4. Willard F. Harley, Jr., *His Needs, Her Needs* (Old Tappan: Fleming H. Revell, 1986), 11.

5. Kevin Cowherd, "Buying Gifts for Women Can Be a Risky Business," *Arkansas Democrat*, 11 April 1989, 4. As quoted in Robert Lewis and William Hendricks, *Rocking the Roles* (Colorado Springs: Navpress, 1991), 83.

Chapter 9

1. Keith Meyering in an interview in "The Small Group Letter," *Discipleship Journal*, Issue 49, 1989, 41.

2. Gordon Dalbey, *Healing the Masculine Soul* (Dallas: Word, 1988), 146.

3. As quoted in Dave Simmons, *Dad the Family Coach* (Wheaton, Ill.: Victor Books, 1990), 32.

4. Robert Bly, *Iron John* (New York: Vintage Books, 1992), 32. Copyright 1990 by Robert Bly.

5. As quoted in Dave Simmons, *Dad the Family Coach*, 31.

Chapter 10

1. As quoted by Robert Lewis and William Hendricks, *Rocking the Roles* (Colorado Springs: Navpress, 1991), 207.

Chapter 11

1. Carol Kuykendall, *Learning to Let Go* (Grand Rapids: Zondervan, 1985), 9.

2. James Dobson, *Parenting Isn't for Cowards* (Dallas: Word, 1987), 209-211.

3. Abstracted from James C. Dobson, *The Strong-Willed Child* (Wheaton: Tyndale House Publishers, 1978). As quoted by Kuykendall, *Learning to Let Go*, 40, and taken from "Setting Your Adolescent Free" (Arcadia: Focus on the Family).

4. Erma Bombeck, *Motherhood, The Second Oldest Profession* (New York: McGraw-Hill, 1983), 30. As quoted in Kuykendall, *Learning to Let Go*, 28.

5. Nancy P. McConnell, "Thoughts on Motherhood" (Colorado Springs: Current, Inc., 1983). As quoted in Kuykendall, *Learning to Let Go*, 39.

6. Dr. Jerry Lewis's address in San Antonio, Texas, as referred to in Delores Curran, *Traits of a Happy Family* (San Francisco: Harper & Row Publishers, 1983), 231.

7. *LA Times*, 18 May 1986.

Chapter 12

1. Michael E. McGill, *The McGill Report on Male Intimacy* (N.Y.: Holt, Rinehart and Winston, 1985), 157-58.

2. As cited in R. Kent Hughes, *Disciplines of a Godly Man* (Wheaton: Crossway Books, 1991), 59.

3. Patrick Morley, *The Man in the Mirror* (Brentwood: Wolgemuth & Hyatt, 1989), 117.

4. As cited in Dr. Ron Jenson, "High Ground Perspectives" (audio tape series), San Diego, Calif., Summer 1992.

5. Harold G. Moore and Joseph L. Galloway, *We Were Soldiers Once...and Young* (New York: Random House, 1992), xiv.

6. Charles Sell as cited by Dr. Ron Jenson, "High Ground Perspectives."

7. David W. Smith, *The Friendless American Male* (Ventura: Regal Books, 1983), 15.

8. Ibid.

9. Ibid.

10. From Stu: "Try as I may, I was unable to locate the original source of this mimeographed handout."

Chapter 13

1. Dr. Ron Jenson, "High Ground Perspectives" (audio tape series), San Diego, Calif., Summer 1992.

2. David W. Smith, *The Friendless American Male* (Ventura: Regal Books, 1983), 14.

3. R. Kent Hughes, *Disciplines of a Godly Man* (Wheaton: Crossway Books, 1991), 61.

Chapter 14

1. Joseph M. Stowell, "The Making of a Man," *Moody Monthly*, May 1992, 4.

2. Ibid.

3. Ibid.